C000199804

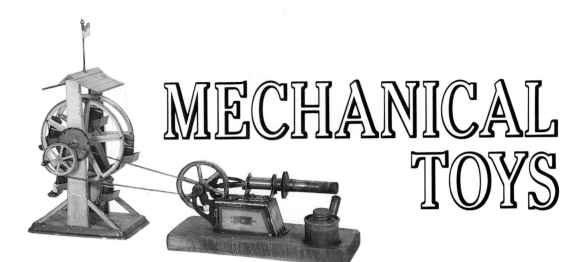

MECHANICAL TOYS

MECHANICAL TOYS

TOYS

HOW OLD TOYS WORK

Athelstan and Kathleen Spilhaus

Photographs by Nelson McClary

CROWN PUBLISHERS, INC.   NEW YORK

All toys illustrated are from the Spilhaus collection.

Line drawings on pages 15, 30, 46, 95, and 107 by John Draves.
Reproduced by permission of Encyclopaedia Britannica, Inc. From *1984
Yearbook of Science and the Future.*

Published by Crown Publishers, Inc., 201 East 50th Street, New York,
New York 10022

CROWN is a trademark of Crown Publishers, Inc.

Manufactured in Japan

Library of Congress Cataloging-in-Publication Data
Spilhaus, Athelstan.
    Mechanical toys: how old toys work / Athelstan Spilhaus and Kathleen
Spilhaus: photographs by Nelson McClary.
    Bibliography.
    Includes index.
    1. Toys, Mechanical—History.   2. Toy making—History.
I. Spilhaus, Kathleen.   II. Title.
TS2301. T7S674   1989
688.7′28—dc19   88-25758
ISBN 0-517-56966-3

Design by June Marie Bennett

10   9   8   7   6   5   4   3   2   1

First Edition

Contents

How It All Started

During World War I, my family was interned in the then British colony of South Africa because my father was a German national. Therefore, between the ages of three and ten, I lived on a farm eighty miles from the nearest railroad station. We had few toys except those that I, my black friends, and Afrikaans neighbors made ourselves. We sawed wheels from round logs and saved precious wooden crates as well as the nails which held them together to make oxcarts. Our black playmates, with their artistic sense, fashioned the oxen to draw the carts from river clay baked in the sun. These were my toys.

Later, when the war was over and I returned with my family to Capetown, I was given a Meccano set. This gift probably fixed the course of my life. I could construct and invent things, and decided to be an engineer at the age of ten. The beautiful thing about Meccano was that you could add to it. For pennies, you could buy an extra gear or an eccentric cam. I once won a prize by sending one of my Meccano inventions for an ice-making machine to *Meccano* magazine. My father had been responsible for the first ice-making company in South Africa. I went to the university to study engineering as a result of this toy. At that time, the only toy I had was a 1913 Model T to take me backward up the mountain to school because the gravity feed of the car would not work the other way.

I forgot about toys in my studies of the real world of engineering, and it was only after finishing my studies at M.I.T. that my interest was reawakened by a beautiful automaton, a drinking bear, which my wife's grandmother had given her. It drank continuously, reminding me of the Grimm fairy tale of the milk jug that was always full. It had probably been purchased about 1880. It did not work very well and, knowing nothing about toys at that time, we tried to fix it. This probably launched me into my lifelong love of antique mechanical toys. I now realize that my attempt to repair the bear in 1936 probably did more harm than good, but with the experience gained over the last fifty years I have again worked on it and it is at last returned to its former glory. Both I and the bear will drink to that.

Everybody asks when I started collecting toys. The drinking bear, an early Decamps, circa 1860, was the beginning. I thank my former wife, Mary, and my later helpmates, Gail and Kathy, for encouraging me in this lasting excursion into the enchanting world of miniature mechanical marvels.

ATHELSTAN SPILHAUS

MECHANICAL TOYS

1. Witch stirring cauldron. Clockwork. English, circa 1920.

1

The Enchantment of Toys

Defined as things that provide pleasure and are not essential to physical well-being, toys mean many things to many people.

The word *toy* may come from the Dutch *tuig*—tools, things, or stuff—or from the Danish *tover*—to stay, to tarry. Large or miniature, caricatures or lifelike models, dynamic mechanical toys to be put into action or static toys to be admired—the variety is almost limitless. Toys give joy to everyone—not just children. From dolls to diamonds, teddy bears to video games, robots to sports cars, a toy

2. Jack-in-the-box. Lithographed paper on wood. Victorian.

is anything that enables us to pleasantly tarry from the fast whip of ordinary life.

The Appeal of Toys

A toy's appeal lies in the form and shape, the beauty of line, the color and detail, the charm of miniaturization, and the humor of caricature. Some toys amuse us with their jerky antics; others add beauty to our lives with their grace and rhythm. Many do things we can't do in real life, thereby keeping us in touch with fantasy. They can bring a whole menagerie onto a table, exotic characters into your hand. Terror is evoked by little witches (figure 1) or jack-in-the-boxes (figure 2). By taking the place of the real thing, which is usually unobtainable, toys stimulate the imagination and satisfy our very human desire for play.

History in Toys

Toys faithfully reflect the society of their time as a whole. If they didn't, they wouldn't sell. They record the hopes, fears, and prejudices of their times and, unlike our textbooks, are safe from revisionist historians. Aeronautical and space toys, often predating actual engineering in the real world, symbolize man's aspiration to fly in the air and the universe. Miniature armies, models of engines of destruction, and mechanized monsters mirror humankind's warlike nature. Stereotyped black dancers (figures 3 and 4) and minstrels, Uncle Tom

3. Black dancers. Ives, American, circa 1890.

4. Mechanism of the Ives dancers.

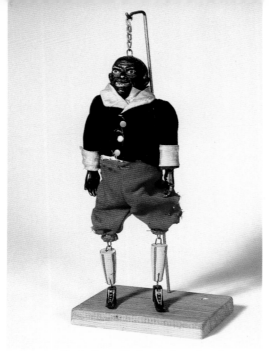

dancing at the end of a rope (figure 5), Aunt Jemima dolls, and *Little Black Sambo* stories remind us that racial prejudice was far more blatant around the turn of the century.

A rare and grisly toy of 1791 depicts the hatred of the French peasants for their former rulers. Constructed of lithographed paper on wood and actuated by sand, it is a miniature blacksmith's shop in which figures in revolutionary garb hammer on an anvil and put into a forge the guillotined heads of aristocrats (figure 6). A motto reads, *"Ici on reforges les têtes de familles chez M. Lustucire"*

5. Dancing Uncle Tom. Clockwork. Ives, American, patented March 30, 1886.

6. Guillotined heads in forge. Paper-on-wood sand toy. De Lauze, French, 1791.

7. Sailboat. Ives, American, patented 1901.

8. Napoleon III and parading Zouaves. Clockwork with music. Tin litho and hand-colored paper on wood. Circa 1860.

("Here we restyle the heads of families at Monsieur Lustucire's"). The toy maker, Jean Curé de Ste. Croix de Lauze, signed and dated his work on the back. Since, before the Revolution, toy makers were generally under the patronage of a noble, perhaps de Lauze was making a political statement in an attempt to save his own head.

Most toy makers do not help us by dating their toys, although some toys do carry patent dates, as does the Ives sailboat (figure 7) marked "Patented, October 29, 1901." Other dates can be found in old sales catalogues.

Collections of old things naturally pique an interest in history and may lead to its study. The French forge toy led us to learn more about the gentle practices

9. General Grant smoker. Clockwork. Ives, American, patented October 30, 1877.

10. General Lee. Lithographed tin wind-up. Japanese, circa 1950.

of that bloody period. An attempt to date a toy depicting Legionnaires parading before Napoleon III (figure 8) led to many pleasant hours finding out when the Foreign Legion was started, when Napoleon III came to power (1852), and when the Franco-Prussian War ended his reign (1870). It was also possible to identify the emperor and some of his ministers by comparing the faces in the hand-painted background with pictures in books.

Famous people as well as events have been celebrated in toys. There is General Grant smoking a cigar (figure 9) and General Butler in Confederate uniform produced by Ives not long after the Civil War. A tinplate lithographed toy depicting General Lee on horseback (figure 10) was made in Japan for the American market in the 1950s. President Theodore

11. Moon Mullins and Kayo on handcar. Wind-up. Marx, American, circa 1930.

12. Popeye and Olive Oyl. Tin litho wind-up. Marx, American, circa 1930.

Roosevelt's bear-hunting escapades inspired the beloved teddy bear, originally Teddy's Bear.

Comic Toys

Stage, radio, and comic page characters inspired toys. Shirley Temple dolls, a wind-up Louis Armstrong with his trumpet, the Moon Mullins and Kayo handcar (figure 11), and numerous Popeye toys (figure 12) are but a few. Walt Disney's creations have been delighting children for more than fifty years.

The Yellow Kid, featured in many toys (figure 13), was a minor character, a bald kid in a group of slum children, in the first newspaper comic strip, *Hogan's Alley,* created by Frank Outcault in 1895. The Yellow Kid spoke only through messages scrawled in patois on his yellow

13. Yellow Kid chewing-gum dispenser. Coin-in-the-slot clockwork. Pulver Chemical Co., Rochester, N.Y., patented May 30, 1899.

nightshirt, and became a favorite in the New York *World*. William Randolph Hearst, publisher of the New York *Journal*, hired Outcault to draw a Yellow Kid strip for his newspaper. *Hogan's Alley* continued in the *World*, drawn by another artist. A series of acrimonious lawsuits ensued between the two publishers, both of whom were accused of "yellow journalism," a term which referred to the color of the Kid's shirt.

Dating Toys from History

Often a fair amount of digging into the history books yields exciting inferences.

Lehmann's string-climbing tin balloon with a flag-waving sailor in a gondola was first manufactured in Germany in 1895. Originally called Mars (EPL #400), the name was changed to Luna in 1900 following the success of a German operetta *Dame Luna*, which featured a balloon flight to the moon. Luna remained in production until 1935. The toys intended for export carried the appropriate national colors, those for sale at home, the Lehmann trademark on the flag.[1]

Jupiter (figure 14) has a sailor in a gondola waving an American flag with forty-five stars. This would indicate that the toy was made after 1896, when Utah joined the Union, and before 1907, when Oklahoma became the forty-sixth state. Jupiter's gondola is octagonal, as is the one used for Mars, suggesting that it is an early model.

However, unlike Mars and Luna, the Lehmann trademark is not printed on the balloon. This may not have been unusual in toys intended for export. Later, when anti-German sentiments were running high before, during, and after World War I, many German toys were deliberately left unmarked.

Learning from Toys

All good toys are inherently educational. The best teach subliminally while you are having fun with them; the worst are labeled educational and never get off the ground. For safety considerations, tin toys that cut children's fingers have lately been banned from toy shops, to be replaced by plastic. The old tin toys at least taught children to be careful so as not to cut their fingers!

We learn from toys how little the amusements of children have changed; how little the amusements of adults differ from those of children, except for purity of delight; and how toys are the additive to preserve our childish enchantment with magic, wonder, and play. Toys were never just for children. Those who contemplate toys are temporarily able to forget some of the constraints of the real world. For brief periods, we can escape murky reality and return to pure fantasy, listening for the toys' unspoken simple commentary on problems and prejudices, loves and frustrations.

14. Jupiter balloon. Pull-string operated. Lehmann, German, circa 1905.

15. Clown balancing on ball automaton. Cloth dressed, clockwork. French, circa 1890.

2
Early
Toy
Inventors

It is difficult to distinguish between engineering innovators and toy makers; both leaven their practical ingenuity with a healthy measure of fantasy (figure 15). Similarly, it is sometimes hard to draw the line between an innovative toy and the workaday world. The brilliant engineers of ancient Greece used their scientific discoveries relating to the properties of rising hot air, compressed air, and columns of water to animate statues, mysteriously cause doors to open and close, and enable artificial birds to fly and sing. Although some of these mechanisms may not have been toys in the conventional

16. Serinette, hand-cranked pipe organ. Wooden gears and inlaid box, lever bellows, tin pipes. Jon Guillaume à Mirecourt en Lorraine, French, circa 1740.

sense, they doubtless lifted the spirit and gladdened the heart. These ingenious devices, while not essential to physical well-being, provided pleasure to both the innovator and the viewer.

In these devices, the engineering principles newly discovered by the Greeks were first put to practical use. Hero of Alexandria invented an engine, a spherical boiler whirled by steam jets, two thousand years ago. The mysteriously opening temple doors and singing artificial birds of Hellenic times were water-actuated, but toys moved by falling water are uncommon, probably because they are messy and subject to rust. Hero also devised a pipe organ driven by the wind and a coin-in-the-slot holy water dispenser, a forerunner of modern "one-armed bandits," of arcade amusements, and of vending machines that dispense the holy water of today, Coke. It even might be classified with the mechanical banks of the last century.

The Chinese independently had devised water clocks with crude escapements that kept the hours fairly regularly. Whether the escapement came from Europe to China in the Middle Ages is questionable. Certainly the lodestone, the earliest magnet, came from China, as did fireworks and rockets worked by gunpowder, which were used there thousands of years before the Space Age. There is an authentic account of a brave Chinese who strapped a rocket to the back of a chair mounted on a sled and attempted to propel himself. By blowing himself to bits he blazed the way to Colonel Stapp's record-breaking rocket-sled rides on the Bonneville Salt Flats.

The devices of the ancient Greeks, Egyptians, and Chinese as well as the advances of clockmakers in the Middle Ages were the precursors of many practical mechanical applications. In addition, the marvelous clocks of the Middle Ages were in part toys; the processions of figures and concerts of music that occurred at intervals were certainly as important as the counting of the hours.

Music in Toys

Musical devices, from the singing birds of the ancient Greeks, through the development of pipe organs and carillons often associated with medieval clocks which also included automata, to the perfection of the miniaturized music box by the Swiss at the end of the seventeenth century, have been used by toymakers throughout the ages.

The serinette, a little hand-operated barrel organ that plays high notes from tiny organ pipes (figures 16 and 17), was used by ladies of the eighteenth century to teach canaries to sing. The great nineteenth-century illusionist Eugene Robert-Houdin built an automaton, The Serinette Lesson, depicting a young lady winding her serinette, after which a mechanical bird sings.[2] Canaries, when taken out of their natural environment, will not sing unless they hear singing. Therefore, the serinette was a necessary device. A modern canary breeder asserts that the only way to tell the sex of a young canary is to teach it to sing. Since only the males sing and therefore command a higher price, it is incumbent on

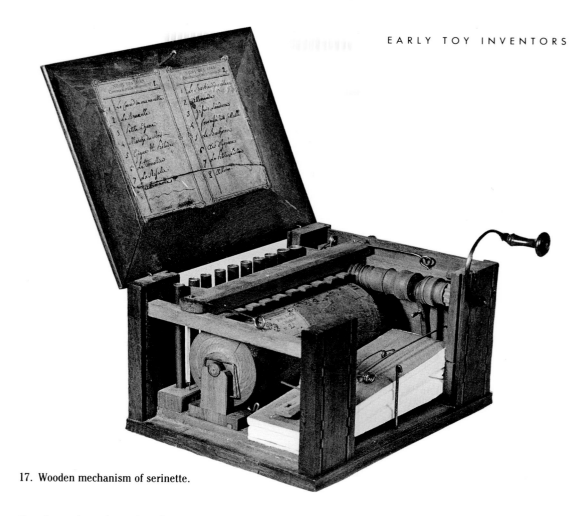

17. Wooden mechanism of serinette.

the breeder to make them sing as early as possible. The modern counterpart of the serinette is tape-recorded birdsong.

Lifelike Toys—Automata

The early automata—complicated, expensive, ingenious—were handmade as one or very few of a kind.

Automata of the eighteenth and nineteenth centuries were programmed by intricate cams to execute complicated series of movements. The length and complexity of the series distinguishes the automaton from the simpler mechanical toy. Complex automata included

lifelike, life-size figures that drew pictures, performed magic tricks, engaged in games of chess, and played musical instruments. The inventors of these princely toys of the eighteenth century are often forgotten.

A nine-inch-tall monkey with clockwork in his torso (figure 18) touches his brush to a palette, paints a brushstroke, peers at his masterpiece, then turns his head for admiration. The painting on the easel is of Benjamin Franklin, sitting for his portrait and surrounded by courtiers in an elegant Parisian salon. So we have a monkey painting a picture of an artist

18. Monkey artist. Cloth dressed, clockwork. French, circa 1870.

19. Boy violinist. Satin dressed, clockwork with music. Vichy, French, circa 1880.

painting a picture of Benjamin Franklin!

In the nineteenth century, the inventors' creations were simplified and made in greater numbers at less expensive prices for a slightly broader market, but still not for children. A boy violinist made by Vichy, a Parisian maker of automata in the late nineteenth century (figure 19), is dressed in the costume of an earlier age with satin knee breeches and flowing golden locks. He sits on a box that contains the clockwork and a fine musical movement. The clockwork causes him to bow the violin while a complicated air is played.

Toy Magicians

A favorite gambit was the shell game, which appears in many forms. In one French automaton of the 1850s (figure 20), the arms of a gypsy are lifted by clockwork cams to expose, as if by magic, different combinations of objects and colors on the table as cups (cones) in the figure's hands are raised and lowered. The legerdemain on the spindly legged table is accomplished by rotating ratchet wheels in the tabletop, activated by a fine wire passing up through one of the table's legs (figure 21).

A much finer and older shell game player (figure 23) has, in addition to the hand-lifting mechanism and the changing of the objects under the cups, multiple movements of the head and eyes. The provenance states that it was built in about 1825 by Louis Rochat of Le Brassus, near Geneva, Switzerland. The elaborately dressed magician performs in a bower of silk camellias.

Automata That Write and Draw

A machine to draw pictures is simpler than a machine to write letters and words. Friedrich von Knauss constructed the most perfect of the mechanical writing automata of his time. His fourth and last writer was presented to the emperor of Austria on October 4, 1760.[3] It wrote a passage of sixty-eight words in French.

Pierre Jacquet-Droz and his apprentices, Jean Frederick Leschot and Henri Maillardet, worked in Geneva in the 1780s. They produced a number of toy writers and draftsmen, including at least two that could both draw and write.

The automata of Jacquet-Droz were presented in every court in Europe in the late eighteenth century. One of these was given to the Chinese court and may still be in Peking today. A document from the

20. Gypsy shell game. Clockwork with music. Probably Lambert, French, circa 1890.

21. Diagram of gypsy shell game mechanism.

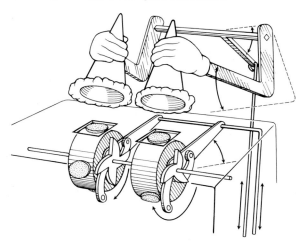

22. Peacock. Real feathers, clockwork. Roullet, Paris, French, 1878.

London Patent Office states that "a copy of the draftsman made by Jacquet-Droz himself and bought at a colossal price for the King of England . . . was sent to Lord Macartney, 1792, on the occasion of his mission to China as a compliment to the Chinese Emperor."[4]

Another automaton, also thought to be the work of Jacquet-Droz, found its way many years later to the Franklin Institute in Philadelphia in a state of terrible dishabille. After painstaking restoration, it was able to reveal the real name of its maker through its own writing. One of its verses is signed, "Written by Maillardet's Automaton." The kneeling figure at a writing desk produces four fine pieces of writing in French and English and three landscape drawings. Although Maillardet had dressed the figure as a young man, the restorers reclothed it as a young girl in bonnet and skirt.[5]

Roullet and Decamps

Jean Roullet began building automata and mechanical toys in Paris in 1866. After his chief assistant, Ernest Decamps, married Roullet's daughter, the firm became Roullet and Decamps in 1889.[6]

In the transition period between the princely toys and mass production, the firm produced fine automata of people and especially animals. A fabulous clockwork peacock (figure 22) was presented in 1878 which walks along, cocks its head, and periodically spreads and closes its tail of real peacock feathers. It has been attributed to Droz, but is illustrated in the first catalogue of Roullet and Decamps.[7]

23. Magician shell game. Fine clockwork and music. Louis Rochat, Geneva, circa 1825.

24. The Artist. Hand-painted face, hat, and hands, spirit-painted body. James Walker, Birmingham, English, 1880.

3 Toward Mass Production

The simplest hobby horse, a broomstick with a toy horse's head on it, was galloped by children rich in imagination but poor in coin. By contrast, in the complex automata of lifelike, life-size dolls, the imagination was in the toy maker and the coin in the princely personage's purse.

Various automata were built during the nineteenth century, but none in sufficient quantity to be what we would call toys, since mass production of mechanical toys did not begin until the latter part of the century. The distinction between automata and mechanical toys is simply the length and complexity of the series of motions performed.

Toy Artists

One such mass-produced automaton prized by collectors is Philip Vielmetter's Artist (figure 25). It is a lithographed tin drawing clown, circa 1895, which is well known and extensively documented. Made in Germany, the crank-operated figure sketches a picture, the X–Y position of his pencil controlled by a double cam that could be changed to draw different designs. One side of the double cam moves the pencil lead in an X (horizontal) direction and the other side of the cam moves the stylus in the Y (vertical) direction (figure 26).

Charles Bartholomew recognized that Vielmetter's clown works on the same principle as its ancestor, Pierre Jacquet-Droz's artist automaton.[8] Until quite recently, it was considered that Vielmetter's genius at simplification made his Artist the first drawing automaton produced in quantity, but this is not the case. The forgotten inventor who preceded Vielmetter by a decade and a half was an Englishman.

A toy also called The Artist (figure 24) is identical in mechanical construction to Vielmetter's but is obviously earlier. The figure has a very simply molded body, not of a clown but of a male artist in suit and hat. It is mostly spirit-painted with hand-painted face, hat, and hands. The registered trademark printed on the box and embossed on the bottom plate of the toy is "J.W.B." It was manufac-

25. Clown artist. Lithographed tin, hand-cranked. Vielmetter, German, 1895.

26. Clown artist mechanism showing double cam.

27. Teddy the Artist. Battery-operated tin litho, showing simple single cams. Japanese, 1960.

28. Zilotone. Heavy sheet metal, tin litho figure, showing double cam. Wolverine, No. 48, Pittsburgh, American, circa 1930.

tured by James Walker of Birmingham in about 1880. Possibly the firm did not prosper and sold its patent to the German, Vielmetter, who changed the figure and embossed it with his own mark on the base.

The cams for the Walker artist are stamped "Made in England," but they work in Vielmetter's clown, and the later Vielmetter cams, stamped "Made in Germany," work in the Walker artist. The operating instructions for the clown are printed in seven languages and the English translation is identical to the directions printed on the box of Walker's artist.

There have been drawing toys since, right up to Teddy the Artist, a battery-operated Japanese toy of the 1950s that draws nine different pictures.[9]

Teddy (figure 27) is a very poor successor to the princely automata and the fine mechanical artists of the past. It is merely a pantograph, reproducing the shape of a cam directly; the cam is nothing more complicated than a circle deformed into the outline of an animal. The ingenious double cam of the older toys, one swinging the pencil horizontally, the other vertically, was not employed. The contemporary designers failed to benefit from the genius of the forgotten inventors.

However, the double cam was used in the Zilotone, an ingenious musical toy of a clown playing real tunes on a xylophone (figure 28). Here, one cam positioned the hammer over the note while the other cam triggered the strike. Numerous interchangeable cams were

29. Democratic Decision Maker. Arcade cast-iron penny-in-the-slot automaton. American, circa 1930.

30. Decision Maker mechanism showing tension springs and rack-and-pinion power mechanism with fly fan.

available for tunes such as "The Farmer in the Dell" and "My Old Kentucky Home."

Political Automata

Two complex mass-produced automata poke fun bipartisanly, and were arcade penny-in-the-slot toys of the Roaring Twenties.

The satin-robed Democratic Decision Maker (figures 29 and 30) is a two-foot-tall cast-iron donkey seated atop a four-foot pedestal. When a penny is inserted into the machine, the rack extends two

helical springs which, governed by a fly fan, provide the power. With seven cams rotated by a rack-and-pinion gear, it chatters its mouth, waggles its ears, nods and turns its head, lifts its arm, and peers through its monocle, then rotates its elbow to spin the wheel of chance. The wheel spins—odd or even—peace or war! The wheel stops, the decision is wrong! The donkey chatters its mouth once more to explain the decision away. Equal time must be given to the Republican elephant which, by stereotype more erudite, riffles the pages of a book until

31. A Good Joke. Lithographed paper and clockwork, wood frame. Schoenhut, American, circa 1890.

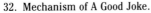

32. Mechanism of A Good Joke.

an equally random decision is picked out by its trunk.

Living Pictures

Animated or "living" pictures made by Schoenhut, a Philadelphia toy maker, adorned Victorian walls. In one entitled A Good Joke (figures 31 and 32), two clerics enjoying their wine move their arms and jaws while rocking with laughter. Concealed behind the lithograph is an array of clockwork, string belts, cardboard cams, and wire levers with counterbalancing weights. The scene is animated by a belt-driven cam from a slow-moving shaft in the clockwork while the highest-speed axle carries a fast-moving fan that acts as a governor. Other patterns for living pictures were provided on flat, lithographed printed sheets to be cut out and animated according to the pleasure of the assembler (figures 33 and 34).

Phonograph Toys

When Thomas Edison's marvelous phonograph was adapted so that it could use flat records instead of cylinders, toy designers quickly saw their chance to add animated figures powered by the rotation

33. *Laboratoire du Restaurant,* "*AU LAPIN SANS TÊTE.*" Animated picture. Pellerin & Cie., French, circa 1900.

34. "*AU LAPIN SANS TÊTE.*" Uncut picture with instructions for home assembly.

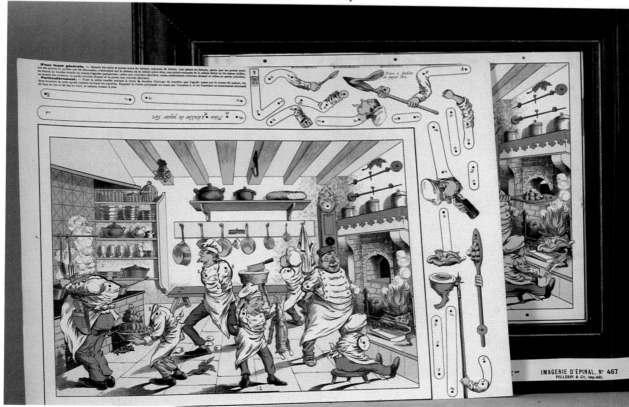

35. Uncle Sam and the Kaiser, Uncle Sam and Pancho Villa. Phonograph toys. American, circa 1916.

36. Siam Soo. Clothed wooden phonograph dancer. American, 1909.

of the record. The choice was large, from the 1909 Siam Soo (figure 36), who made exotic Balinese dancing motions in time to a fast fox trot, to fighting cocks and black pugilists. One such toy (figure 35) features Uncle Sam and Mexican guerrilla leader Pancho Villa. Villa is being punished by repeated kicks from Uncle Sam for instigating a Mexican-U.S. border incident in 1916. When the United States entered World War I, Villa was replaced by a bomb-carrying version of Kaiser Wilhelm II of Germany.

Tin Toys

The earliest mechanical tin toys were probably made by Hess in Germany. The Hess company was founded in Nürnberg in 1826. Hess's son took over the firm in 1866. It may have been Hess that originated or at least used the inertial flywheel engine, a feature of what were called Hessmobile cars.

In America, George Whitfield Brown, a clockmaker of Forestville, Connecticut, began producing the toys that his family considered a hobby sideline to the manufacture of clocks in 1854. Thus, the works of inexpensive clocks were incorporated into toys to give them motion. Brown is credited with the first mass-produced mechanical toy activated by clockwork, in 1856.

Toys That Walk

The autoperipatetikos (figures 37 and 38) is said to be the first mechanical toy patented in America of which there are examples extant. Invented by Enoch Rice Morrison and patented July 15, 1862, it appeared in a number of variations. The most common was a doll with a wax, china, or composition head wearing a full skirt which concealed the mechanism. The toy was also produced with a more slender body as the Walking Zouave, and as a doll for the English market. The most ingenious parts are the projections under the shoes that alternately protrude and engage the surface while the other foot slides forward with the projection retracted.

The autoperipatetikos was widely sold in Europe as well as in America. The same system of walking was later used by Fernand Martin and others in Europe.

A Famed American Toy Maker

Edward R. Ives began manufacturing hot-air toys in 1866 and moved his business to Bridgeport, Connecticut, four years

37. Autoperipatetikos. Walking doll in silk gown. Morrison, American, patented 1862.

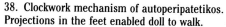

38. Clockwork mechanism of autoperipatetikos. Projections in the feet enabled doll to walk.

39. Secor piano player. Wood, cast iron, clockwork with music. Ives, American, circa 1885.

later. The firm of Ives and Blakeslee was to dominate the American toy scene for several decades.

At about the same time, Ives collaborated with an extremely ingenious inventor, Jerome Secor, his next-door neighbor, who was producing sewing machines. Secor's Bridgeport Toy Company was housed in Ives's factory and later sold to Ives. In 1880, Secor's stationery (figure 45) advertised artificial singing birds, The American Warblers, as well as cannons and toy pistols and "clock movements for toys." About a half dozen of the most-prized American toys were designed for Ives by Secor.[10]

Secor designed the first cast-iron clockwork locomotive and the Freedman Bank. His piano player (figure 39) first appeared with an imported French bisque head, later replaced by cast metal. The fact that the figure's arms

40. Secor tambourine player. Cast iron on wood base, clockwork. Ives, American, circa 1885.

41. Mechanism of tambourine player.

42. Secor's Brudder Bones. Cast iron and wood, clockwork. Ives, American, circa 1885.

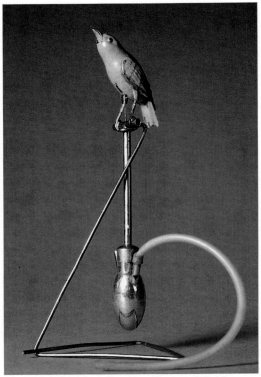

43. Secor's American Songster. Brass and tin. Ives, American, circa 1885.

were attached to its waist rather than its shoulders was concealed by a flowing gown. There were also three black minstrels playing different instruments—tambourine (figures 40 and 41), banjo, and bones (figure 42).

A very rare toy called Sister Lucinda at the Play was, until recently, known only from an old Ives catalogue. The old black woman, with the same mechanism as the minstrels, fans herself with a palm leaf, taps her foot, and sways in obvious enjoyment of the minstrels' entertainment. The only extant example of this toy was recently acquired by a California collector.

Pneumatics and Hydraulics

An extension of the Greeks' use of pneumatics and hydraulics is seen in The American Songster, designed for Ives by Secor (figure 43). When air that is blown into a mouthpiece bubbles through water in the egg-shaped reservoir at the bottom of the bird's perch, the bird bursts into song. A piston in the air cylinder above the reservoir oscillates a wire that extends up the hollow perch and moves the bird's tail and bill. Both motion and tune are modulated by the bubbles as air is forced through the water.

"Highly appreciated by ladies," said

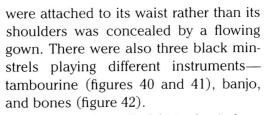

Ives in its 1913 catalogue, "who use it to teach birds to sing. . . . When used near a bird will induce it to start up its best notes immediately." This recalls the serinette of more than a century before.

A lithographed tinplate German singing bird (figures 46 and 47) is only the size of a small thrush, yet internal clockwork drives a remarkable array of mechanisms. A piston bellows blows a tiny flute similar to a Suwannee whistle (a nineteenth-century bird whistle). A cam moves the stop to vary the notes of the song. Other levers make the bird flap its wings and tail, turn its head, and open and close its beak.

The General Grant Smoker (figure 9), patented by Ives in 1877, featured a cam-operated piston that pulls smoke in from a small cigar while a lever lowers the general's hand and the piston expels smoke through his mouth.

Ives made many less complicated clockwork toys, including a monkey churning and a woman churning butter (figure 44).

The Industrial Revolution turned toy making into big business. Toys were now made by mass production. The actuating mechanisms, instead of being good clockwork, were much more cheaply produced spring-run gears with crude escapements.

Restoration and Throw-aways

Many of the best toy collectors and dealers handle only toys in the finest original condition. This, of course, is admirable and understandable, but if one is interested in the working of toys,

44. Woman churning butter. Cloth dressed, clockwork. Ives, American, circa 1895.

45. Jerome Secor's letter and letterhead. Dated August 14, 1880.

46. Thrush. Lithographed tin singing bird, clockwork. German, circa 1920.

47. Diagram of mechanism of thrush.

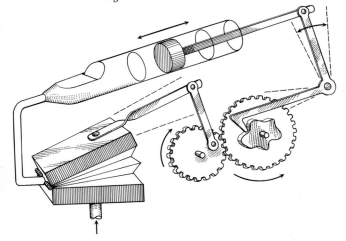

surely it is better to have an example not in perfect condition than to not have one at all. We consider repairs to mechanisms to make the toy work important and allowable, but we do not recommend cosmetic restoration. Although repainting old toys is becoming more acceptable among collectors—and obviously it is the prerogative of the owner —we feel that repainting is irreversible. Should a repainted toy be passed on to someone else, that person's choice is limited: The toy cannot be "unrepainted." It is said that the famous collector and writer Louis Hertz would not even brush cobwebs off!

In the days when real machines were built to last, be repaired, and last again, most toys were manufactured in quantity with no thought of repair. Hand-painted toys were soldered, and later lithographed tin toys were held together with bent tabs. Neither was designed to be repaired; resoldering destroyed the delicate hand-painted colors, and the metal tabs broke off by fatigue if the toys were taken apart—certainly a foreshadowing of today's throw-away culture.

This throw-away culture has led, since the 1950s, to the dominance of plastic and battery-operated toys. Think of all the batteries that have to be thrown away shortly after Christmas!

4
What Toys Were Made Of

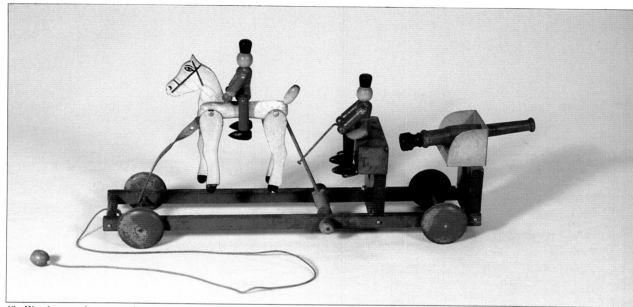

48. Wooden cavalryman and gun. Pull toy.

Before the plastic age in toys—no matter how long before, thousands of years before—toys, not being essential to survival or physical well-being, were made either of the most common things at hand in their particular locality or of keepsake materials, the most prized available. In the Stone Age, undoubtedly, stones naturally rounded in a rapidly flowing river were used as playthings and, indeed, the counters in very early games of chance were pebbles or seeds. The dice were knucklebones of animals.

49. Battleship *Philadelphia* with sailors and rum kegs. Paper litho on wood. Reed, American, circa 1880.

Wood, Paper, and Iron

Later on, for the common toys, in the Schwartzwald, the Black Forest of Germany, wooden toys abounded (figure 48) and even wooden-geared clocks, like the cuckoo clocks that are still resisting the invasion of plastic. With the invention of inexpensive color lithographing on paper, beautiful paper litho-on-wood toys were made.

The materials used in the manufacture of toys were the most inexpensive that could be found—wood, lithographed paper (figure 49), tin (figure 51), and, in America, cast iron. When the iron and steel industry burgeoned, particularly in Pennsylvania and in the industrial northeastern United States, beautiful archetypical American toys made of cast iron appeared. Generally these were banks and horse-drawn vehicles (figures 50 and 55), but there were also cast-iron locomotives and early automobiles (figure 53), a few actuated by clockwork. Jerome Secor used cast-iron pieces for his creations.

Toy makers of other countries used the cheapest materials available to them in the manufacture of their toys. Only in England, where the iron and steel industry was highly developed in the Midlands, do we see cast-iron toys.

50. Horse-drawn brake. Hand-painted cast iron. American, circa 1890.

Tin Toys

Tin toys, the common name universally used, are not tin at all but generally thin sheets of rolled iron or steel (figure 52). In the earliest examples of toys like these, tin, being the most ductile metal, was used; hence the name. Since tin was expensive, it was soon replaced by cheaper materials, but the toys were still called tin in common parlance.

After the tin can was invented in the early nineteenth century, tin toys were commonly manufactured from recycled food containers. It is interesting that, after great wars both in Germany and Japan and elsewhere, one can find toys

51. *Tiger* locomotive. Hand-painted tin, clockwork. George Brown, American, circa 1880.

52. Musicians on park bench and clown playing clarinet. Hand-painted tin, clockwork with fly fan, plinkety-plink music. Gunthermann, German, circa 1880.

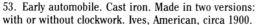

53. Early automobile. Cast iron. Made in two versions: with or without clockwork. Ives, American, circa 1900.

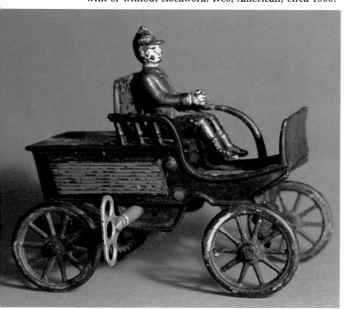

lithographed on the visible side but with the labeling showing the original use of the can on the inside.

Aluminum and Celluloid

Two materials of comparatively modern invention are aluminum and celluloid. Aluminum, the most modern of common metals, was first purified in 1825 and shown to the public thirty years later at the Paris Exposition of 1855. It is the third most abundant element on the earth's surface after oxygen and silicon. One would think that a metal in such abundance, next to the constituents of the air we breathe and the earth we tread on, would have been one of the first to be used by man. The reason it came into use so late was that it never is found in metallic form in nature. It occurs in the form of aluminum salts, such as aluminum oxide, and in rocks or weathered rocks (earth and soil) in the form of aluminum silicate (clay). It cannot be produced by the smelting of ores as can such other common metals as iron, copper, zinc, lead, gold, or silver.

Even after the middle of the last century, aluminum was used in few toys. One toy kept us baffled because, although obviously old, the figure, reminiscent of the early New England limberjacks, was of cast aluminum, with a cast-iron base (figure 54). The limberjack, a figure with jointed arms and legs, was one of the earliest toys made in

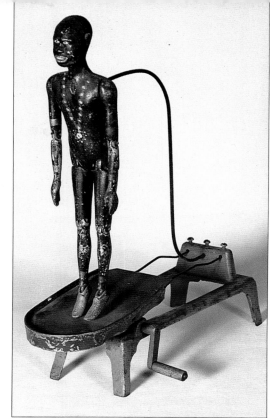

54. Dancing Negro. Cast-aluminum figure, cast-iron base, hand-cranked. American, date unknown (1890–1920).

55. Hearse. Hand-painted cast iron, wooden coffin. American. This macabre toy may have been one of a kind.

56. Foxhunt wind-up. Celluloid fox, dogs, and mounted hunter on tin base. Japanese, 1930s.

57. *Les Acrobats* gravity toy. Composition tumblers on wire frame, made in several versions with either two or four acrobats. French, circa 1920.

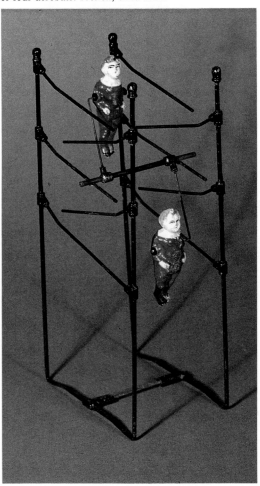

America. It was generally of wood with a rod running into the back of the figure and a flat board on which it danced. The rod and the end of the board were held against each other, and vibrated to make the figure dance.

This jointed metal figure is obviously not pure aluminum but aluminum with quite a large percentage of silicon, since casting pure aluminum is very difficult. It is a fortunate happenstance that, when you partially purify aluminum silicate and leave about 10 percent of the silicon in it, it casts nicely, whereas pure aluminum is cast only with extreme difficulty. So we do see old toys with cast-aluminum silicon alloy parts.

On the other hand, pure aluminum, because of its softness and high ductility, is easily rolled, forged, and drawn. One would think that pure aluminum sheet might have been used instead of tin for the full-blown figure of what we call tin toys. Probably because it cannot easily be soldered and because of its high cost until after World War II, aluminum appears in far fewer toys than one might

36

expect. After that time, when it became cheap, new materials supplanted it.

Celluloid is another fascinating component for toys and a very widely used one. Celluloid was the first synthetic material made of nonmetallic chemicals. It was invented in 1870 by J. W. and I. S. Hyatt, who combined cellulose nitrate (camphor) and alcohol under heat and pressure. Their invention, which bore the U.S. trade name celluloid, was based on earlier British research by A. Parkes and D. Spill.

Celluloid was tough, strong, had a high gloss, was cheap and resistant to water, oils, and other stains, and was easily worked. The white-collar workers who were paid a pittance at the turn of

the century wore shirts with high stiff collars and cuffs to their offices. Very soon collars and cuffs were made of celluloid because they became soiled first and could be detached and washed off with a damp rag, instead of laundering the whole shirt. Wealthier people of those days, who could better afford both shirts and laundry, looked down upon the celluloid-cuff-and-collar class.

But celluloid was, as we say today, thermoplastic. It could be easily pressed in molds at temperatures just above the boiling point of water. It was ideal for cheap dolls and for the figures of mechanical toys, and was used for these widely in many countries, notably in Japan prior to World War II (figure 56).

58. Jungle fight. Hair, fur, and papier-mâché clockwork crocodile, elephant, lion, tiger. Ernest Decamps, French, 1890s; monkey collecting coconuts in palm tree. Tin litho marble gravity toy. Japanese, 1950s.

59. Fur-covered clockwork tiger. Sniffs, crouches, growls, and leaps. Decamps, French, 1890s.

Celluloid could be worked in such thin sheets that the toys were fragile and brittle at low temperatures. Thus, the Japanese celluloid has become rare and is far more prized than the postwar plastics that replaced it. Like tin, which could cut little fingers, extremely flammable celluloid also frightened nervous parents.

Other Materials

Composition, a term used for various materials ground fine and stuck together with glue, was, on the other hand, much less flammable. It was also easily molded and accepted paint readily. Pulverized materials led to pressboard and even good gears of pressed metal (figure 57).

Early toy makers used the materials at hand. For the hair of a doll, they used human hair; for the fur of a toy animal, the skin of some animal. Most notable in this latter regard was Ernest Decamps. In Paris in the 1880s, during the transition from expensive automata to toys made in quantity, he and his father-in-law, Jean Roullet, made toy animals that we marvel at today. With clockwork governed by fly fans and most ingenious lever systems, they perform amazing lifelike antics (figure 58).

The Decamps animals had a power system similar to good clockworks but tending toward mass production. The different lever systems that performed multiple actions were quite varied (figure 61). By and large these power and lever systems were enclosed in papier-mâché bodies which were real sculptures of the shape of the animals.

We also believe, because we have ex-

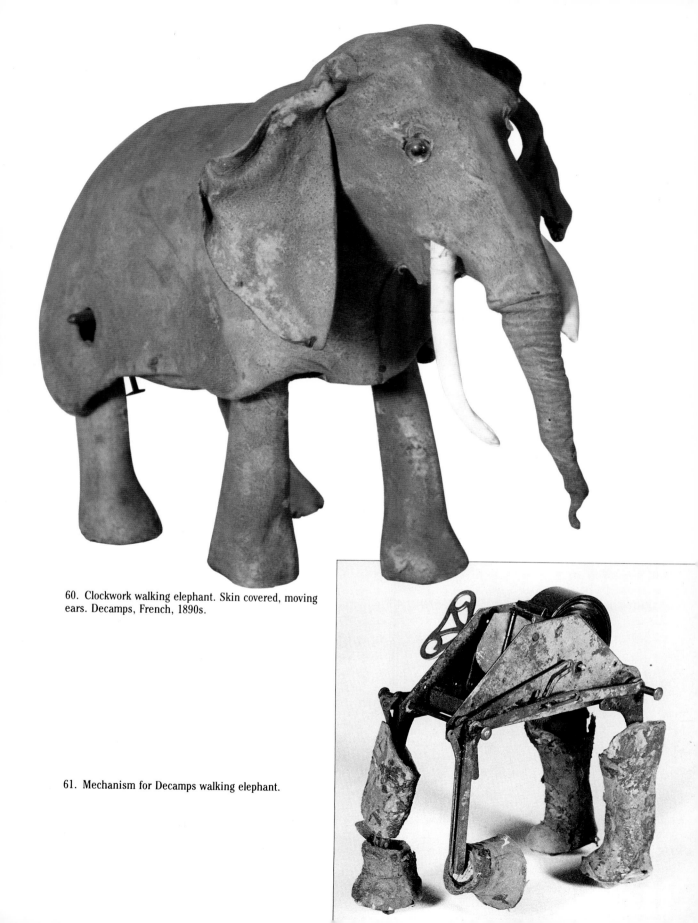

60. Clockwork walking elephant. Skin covered, moving ears. Decamps, French, 1890s.

61. Mechanism for Decamps walking elephant.

amined different animals of the same kind—such as four elephants, three tigers, and two lions, all different in exterior finishing—that these were finished perhaps by some variation of a cottage industry. The elephants had real skin, not elephant skin to be sure, but probably chamois or dog hide. The tigers and lions are covered with short napped animal fur and the lions' manes were variously cat or rabbit fur (figures 59, 60, and 62).

Our prize hen that lays three eggs in a single walk across the table (figure 64) is sheathed in real chicken feathers.

Decamps worked at the height of the French colonial empire in Africa. He represented in toys the exotic beasts of that empire before our era of enlightened preservation of endangered species and unenlightened incineration of abandoned domestic animals.

An Italian toy of the 1920s (figures 65 and 66) is similar to a Decamps but made of metal. Here, unusually, the clockwork mechanism in the horse's body works the feet of the horse and draws the chariot. This is quite different from the more common toy where the wheels of the vehicle drive the feet of the horse.

Toys and Safety

Since children often cut their fingers on tin toys, there are now restrictions on their manufacture and sale. Painted toys must also be made with nontoxic paints, and flammability and toxicity of other

62. Clockwork lion. Fur covered, human hair mane. Opens jaws, roars, crouches, and leaps. Decamps, French, 1890s.

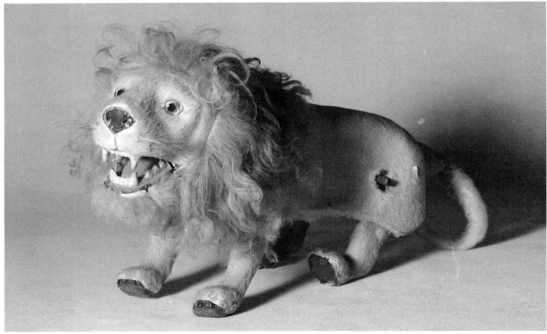

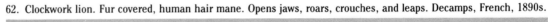

materials is now a concern as well.

We have two examples of an extraordinary gravity toy where a Karakuri tumbler performs three complete backward somersaults down steps (figure 63). The motion is actuated by mercury in the torso, which flows toward the head and causes the figure to turn over backward and land on its hands. The mercury then flows away from the head, causing the lower body to turn over and complete the somersault.

The Karakuri Theater was founded in Japan in 1662 by Takeda Omi, a clock-maker, and continued for more than one hundred years. Performances featured life-sized automata. In 1797, Hosokawa wrote a book called *Karakuri Zui* with

diagrams of the construction of Takeda's automata. From these instructions, miniature toy versions were made, including the Karakuri tumbler.[11]

The delicate wooden figures and the way all the parts fit together into the box that forms the middle step make one believe that this toy was made in Japan. However, there may have been a French version sold in England by W. H. Britain in the latter half of the nineteenth century. Sotheby's May 1988 catalogue lists this toy as circa 1820.

Mercury was an ideal material to actuate the tumbler since it is heavier than lead and is the only metal that is a liquid at ordinary temperatures. It also has the unusual property of not wetting most sur-

63. Karakuri tumbler. Paper and wood gravity toy. Japanese, circa 1820.

64. Feather-covered hen. Walks and lays eggs. Roullet, French, 1878.

65. Roman chariot *Invictus.* Tin litho, clockwork. Sigma, Italian, circa 1920.

66. Mechanism inside Roman chariot horse.

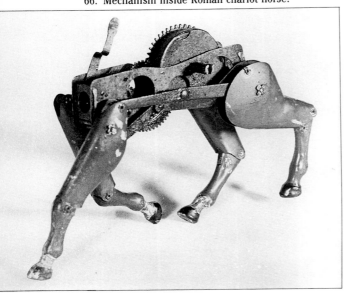

faces, which is why it breaks into little drops on a surface instead of forming a film. Mercury was not often used in toys, probably due to its high price rather than its toxicity, but it was widely used in medicine well into the present century. (It is interesting to note that in the 1911 edition of the Encyclopaedia Britannica, reference is made to swallowing mercury as a cure for constipation!) However, a popular toy of the 1960s, Etch-a-Sketch, did contain mercury and was taken off the market because of it. The latest version of Etch-a-Sketch produced by Ohio Art uses aluminum powder and plastic beads—and does not work as smoothly.

5
Toys That Predicted the Future

67. Corncob roller organ. Hand-cranked. American, circa 1900.

Under a Christmas tree of the 1880s, before toys were made of plastic and powered by electricity, a child could discover the quality of magic—toys that combined reality with fantasy in intriguing and delightful ways.

These traditional toys should hold special fascination for engineers, for they embody, in imaginative applications, many of the principles and devices that are the very stuff of modern machines and structures. Indeed, they often represented the first use of principles and mechanisms that were later widely applied in engineering practice.

68. Ballerinas. Lithographed tin gyro tops, spun by rack on pinion. Einfalt (Kosmos), Cat. #1547, German, 1930s.

From Music Boxes to Computers

Player pianos and music boxes with their punched-roll or spiked-barrel memories were the ancestors of our modern computers. In the so-called corncob organ used in tent churches (figure 67), nails were simply driven into a wooden cylinder which activated the keys of a concertina music mechanism with a bellows pumping the air.

Automata, the princely toys, were programmed by intricate cams to execute series of motions of considerable length and complexity. A cam is a rotating irregular plate that moves a follower held against its edge. The exquisite automata of the seventeenth and eighteenth centuries were the precursors of the programmed tools of the Industrial Revolution and the computerized robots of the modern world.

Games of chance using dice stimulated the development of the science of statistics.

Jets and Rockets

Jet propulsion began with the steam-driven reaction motor devised by Hero of Alexandria. He also used cams to describe the motion of his automata.

Toy boats, called putt-putts because of the noise made when they alternately sucked in water and expelled steam from a heated chamber (figure 69), preceded practical jet propulsion by almost a century.

The first Chinese firecrackers, used for amusement and display, led to the use of gunpowder in weapons and to toy rockets, signal rockets, and, finally, rocket propulsion.

Tops and Gyros

The gyroscope, so important in modern inertial guidance systems, found its first use in one of the most ancient toys, the spinning top (figure 68). Some researchers believe that the top was developed in Japan in the Middle Ages and was brought to Europe by Dutch seamen in the beginning of the sixteenth century.[12]

A toy monorail train (figure 70) traveled upright on a single wheel on a single track using a gyroscope long before Sperry employed gyros in aircraft instruments and to stabilize ocean liners. This toy received patent number 25,732 in En-

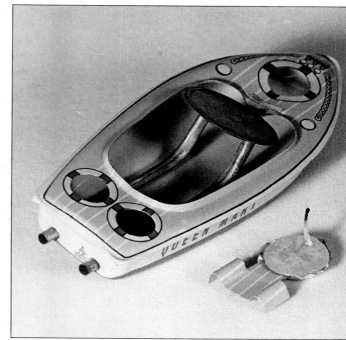

69. Putt-putt boat mechanism. Steam pulse jet. Modern.

70. Gyro Mono-Rail Car. Gyro stabilized and powered single-wheeled vehicle. Ely Cycle Co., British, 1912.

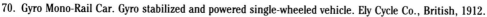

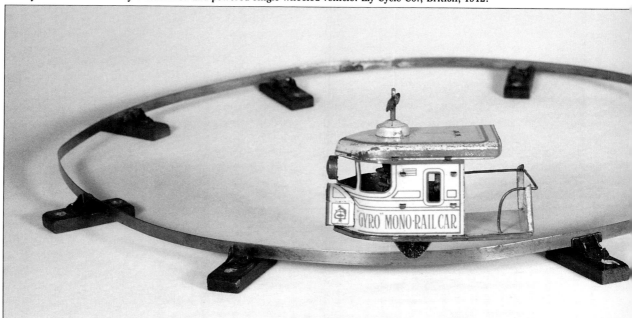

71. Gyrocycle. Tin litho bicycle stabilized and powered by spinning gyro in front wheel. TRI-ANG, British, circa 1950.

72. Ornithopter. Plastic, rubber-band actuated, 1970s.

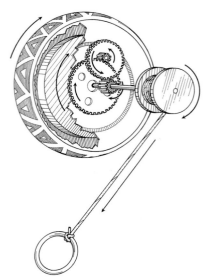

73. Mechanism of gyrocycle.

gland in 1908, and was patented in Germany in 1911 by Reginald Kirby. It was also produced by Suskind in Germany and T. K. in Japan as the horse race jockey top. Much later another British toy, the gyrocycle (figures 71 and 73), a two-wheeled bicycle, traveled upright powered by a spinning gyro on the front wheel.

The Bourdon Tube

The principle of the Bourdon tube, a flattened, flexible tube that straightens out under pressure, was used in pneumatic toys such as the rubber monkey that plays a drum when a rubber bulb is squeezed by hand (figure 74). The Bourdon tube is used today in many steam and other pressure gauges. Compressed air which works the monkey also powers the noisy jackhammers that dig up our streets.

74. Monkey drummer. Rubber, hand-squeezed pneumatic. Modern.

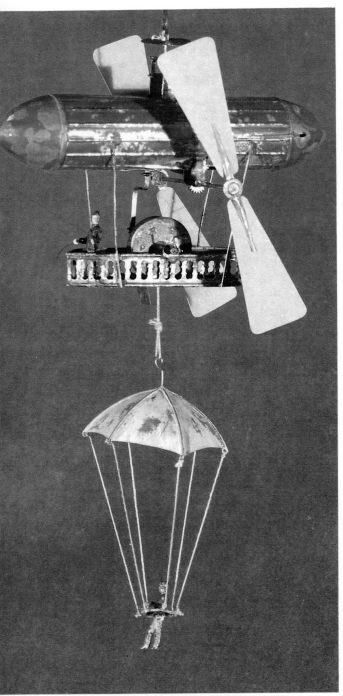

75. Zeppelin with parachute. Hand-painted tin, clockwork. Mueller & Kaederer, German, circa 1890.

76. Balloon with acrobat on trapeze. Hand-painted tin, clockwork. French, circa 1900.

The Bourdon tube is also the underlying principle of the common curled paper party noisemaker which, when blown by mouth, straightens out and incidentally squeals.

From Ornithopter to Powered Flight

As with good science fiction, toys show the shape of things to come, and toy designers found that they could play on people's fantasies.

Toy ornithopters became the embodiment of Leonardo da Vinci's imagination. Modern ones (figure 72) actually fly, although their full-scale counterparts never did.

The brothers Montgolfier discovered in their paper factory that if they trapped heated air in a lightweight paper bag it would float upward. After they sent up their thirty-three-foot hot-air balloon in 1783, balloons immediately claimed the public's fancy and toy makers responded with whimsical creations such as an acrobat cavorting on a trapeze hanging from a balloon (figure 76).

The fantasy of man-powered flight is also suggested by a zeppelin (figure 75), quite impossible in the real world because the propeller propels it sideways. It rises on a string and, when it gets to the top, the pilot, recognizing that the whole contraption is completely impractical, parachutes down.

Reversible Toys

In another hand-painted tin toy (figure 77), four balloons circle and descend a mast. Under each, a man with oars sits in a rowboat. The twirling motion is ac-

77. Balloons with rowboat gondolas. Hand-painted tin, reversible gravity toy. European, circa 1900.

complished by gravity pulling the balloons down the helical screw, which is the mast. This toy is reversible in that it can be turned over to repeat the process.

Another reversible toy is the 1910 Gibbs mechanical seesaw (figure 79). On a vertical strip of corrugated metal, gravity seesaws a boy and girl while pallets at the fulcrum of the seesaw alternately engage the corrugations.

From Optics to Movies

Forerunners of modern cinematography were toys showing animation. Motion was provided mechanically so that the eye could glimpse successive positions of an image. Their names were magical: zoetropes, pantascopes, praxinoscopes, phenakistoscopes, and thaumatropes!

The simplest of these was the thaumatrope (figure 78), which showed just two different positions of a pair of boxers. The earliest ones were twirled by hand. The praxinoscope (figure 80) and zoetrope showed multiple positions before mechanical repetition. The modern motion picture is simply an extension of the number of images before repetition.

Wheels, Balls, and Robots

The first use of the wheel may have been in a toy. A pre-Colombian tribe in Mexico made clay animals on wheels, the only example of the use of the wheel by those people. The ball, originally a round stone and later fashioned crudely from

78. Thaumatrope. Boxer silhouettes on two sides of cards appear to pummel each other when spun by wind-up mechanism. Probably German, circa 1900.

79. Seesaw. Lithographed tin figures, reversible gravity toy. Gibbs, American, circa 1920.

wood or clay and smoothed by use in games, was the precursor of modern ball bearings.

Frequently, toys depicting engines of war preceded the real ones. The ray gun of comic-book hero Buck Rogers antedates modern laser weapons by thirty or forty years. Similarly, Dick Tracy's wrist radio came long before miniaturization of solid-state electronics made beepers, walkie-talkies, and cellular car phones

80. *Le Praxinoscope.* Spirit-painted tin with mirrors on wooden stand, brass candlestick, interchangeable colored moving-picture sequences. ER, Paris, French, 1877.

practical and allowed work to interrupt our playtime. Mechanical robot toys (figure 81) are all humanized. The real robots of industry resemble them not at all.

As early as the 1930s, there were toys that went into action on a voice or hand-clap command, forerunners of many of today's gadgets that turn on lamps and locate lost car keys.

Upside-Down Engineering

That engineering in toys should precede practical engineering in the real world is not at all surprising. Toys inhabit an environment in which they are free from the constraints of "good" engineering practices as well as social responsibility. In other words, toys can do all sorts of things because they do not have to be efficient. In relation to their size, a huge amount of energy can be used to work them. A toy has at its command one whole "child power."

Toys also do not have to run smoothly. In the real world, flywheels are balanced to eliminate vibrations. In toys, however, the forces of vibration either are too small to be destructive or are emphasized to achieve comic effects or to mimic human or animal antics. Less rigorous engineering requirements surely stimulated toy makers to experiment with systems and devices not yet adapted successfully in the real world. Many toys use sudden reversals of movement to surprise and delight. In real life, this

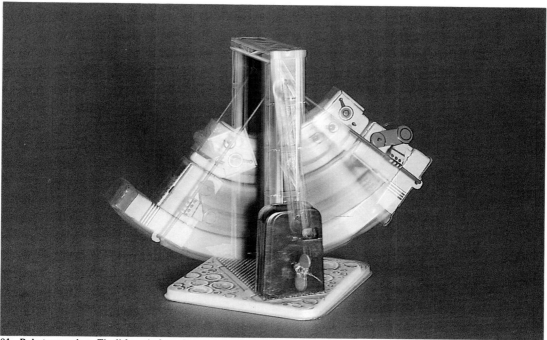

81. Robot on swing. Tin litho wind-up. Yone, Japanese, 1950s.

would be akin to moving forward in your car and then jamming it into reverse.

Toys are abstractions, and toy makers have the same privilege given to cartoonists and caricaturists—of oversimplifying and exaggerating physical characteristics and social relationships.

The material expression of newly discovered physical principles was often an item developed for entertainment. A marvelous example of this is the advent of television (a toy in the sense of its being an entertainment device). Television was an extension of the early motion picture machines that chopped the eye's view mechanically to see a succession of pictures, making it appear as motion. In the motion picture camera, a chopper

blanked the lens while the film advanced one frame. In the earliest television, developed in England by J. L. Baird in 1923, a mechanical chopper was used, called the Nipkow disk. It was superceded by electronic chopping, and television became a great toy before its use for security surveillance and other practical matters. Before the home use of personal computers, video games came about as attachments to television, just as the early phonograph toys came about as extensions of the phonograph.

Someday, our home televisions probably will be programmed to some more useful purpose such as education.

6
Power and Power Storage

82. Boy riding dog. Hand-painted tin, wheeled platform toy. American, circa 1890.

The primary source of power for pre-twentieth-century toys was a child's hand—not only for pushing or pulling (figures 82 and 83), but also for lifting sand or water, raising a weight, winding a spring, pressing an air-filled bulb, or spinning a flywheel. Thus, one of the charms of these toys is that they are hand-sized and hand-energized —handy, one might say. What is more, the hand's energy is stored in the springs, flywheels, and weights of mechanical toys in somewhat the same way that the energy of the sun is stored in wood, coal, and oil.

The Inertial Flywheel

Many old and new toys store energy by spinning a flywheel so that the toy proceeds on its own with friction as the governor. Flywheel storage of energy is now contemplated for slowing down and accelerating buses and subway trains that stop and start frequently.

Storing the energy of the hand in the momentum of a spinning flywheel can be done by spinning the flywheel with a string wound around the axle, as in tops. The flywheel can be spun by hand (figures 85 and 86) or by using an auxiliary spring device (figure 87). The flywheel can also be spun in wheeled floor toys such as engines and automobiles by rubbing the toy along the floor a few times and then letting it go. Collectors often erroneously call them friction-driven toys. Friction, however, cannot drive anything; the preferable term is inertial flywheel-powered. Hillclimbers (figure 84) and Daytons are good examples of older toys that were powered this way, but many modern inexpensive toys still operate with inertial flywheels.

Using Gravity

In gravity toys, sand, marbles, or water are put by hand into an elevated container and work the mechanism as they trickle down. They are the counterparts of hydroelectric power, where falling water generates energy.

Although water wheels have been used for centuries, principally to turn mill wheels, the use of flowing water as a direct source of energy in toys is rare. Rust and messiness constitute obvious

83. Train on wheeled platform. Tin litho pull toy. Georg Levy, Nürnberg, German, 1920s.

84. Car. Wood, tin, cast-iron passengers, inertial flywheel energized by rolling car along surface. Hillclimber, American, circa 1900.

85. Sailboat. Hand-spun inertial flywheel-powered. Tin litho with paper sail and wooden mast. Carette #1038, French, circa 1910.

86. Mechanism of Carette sailboat.

objections to their use. One water-wheel-operated wooden toy of the 1850s used cords, weights, and pulleys to operate a playground scene.[13]

A satisfactory substitute for water was fine sand, as had been used for centuries in hourglasses. The child's hand could lift the dry sand to an elevated hopper from which it trickled down through an orifice to power the turning of the wheel.

Marbles, round lead shot, and ball bearings were also used to power toys. They could fall one by one, adding the additional excitement of a game of chance as they rolled into different indentations in the receptacle at the bottom (figures 89 and 90).

Another method of using gravity as the source of power was to move a single weight upward so that it powered the toy as it descended slowly to the bottom, much as a weight-driven grandfather clock is powered.

In the long-running Newton Aero Circus, a weight in the form of an airship pulls two circling airplanes up a pylon. When they reach the top, the weight is released at the bottom. Ingeniously, the airplanes themselves become the weight and spiral down to a perfect landing (figure 88).

Pneumatic Toys

Flowing air, or wind, used from early times to operate windmills, is used in the simplest of pneumatic toys, the pinwheel. Here the power source is natural wind. Compressed air, used in jackhammers for street repairs, is produced by

87. Press-lever tops. Tin litho, finger-operated rack and spring on pinion spins top. Marx, American, 1930s.

88. Detail of Aero Circus. Gravity-driven aerial toy. Newton, American, 1929.

squeezing a rubber bulb to actuate a toy monkey.

Bubble blowers and smokers are other toys that use pneumatics. In some, like James Walker's bubble blower of 1880 (figure 91), a bellows is activated by hand. Others add clockwork to work the bellows, as in the German smokers (figure 92) and in the Ives General Grant (figure 9).

Another pneumatic toy is the squeak toy. An animal in a cage springs out and makes a noise when the door of the cage is opened. Squeak toys may be operated directly by hand, or the hand may simply close the door against a spring which, when the catch is released, flies open and squeaks as a bellows blows through a noisemaker (figure 93).

We have not dealt with mechanical banks only because they are a specialized collection about which so many good books have been written.[14] How-

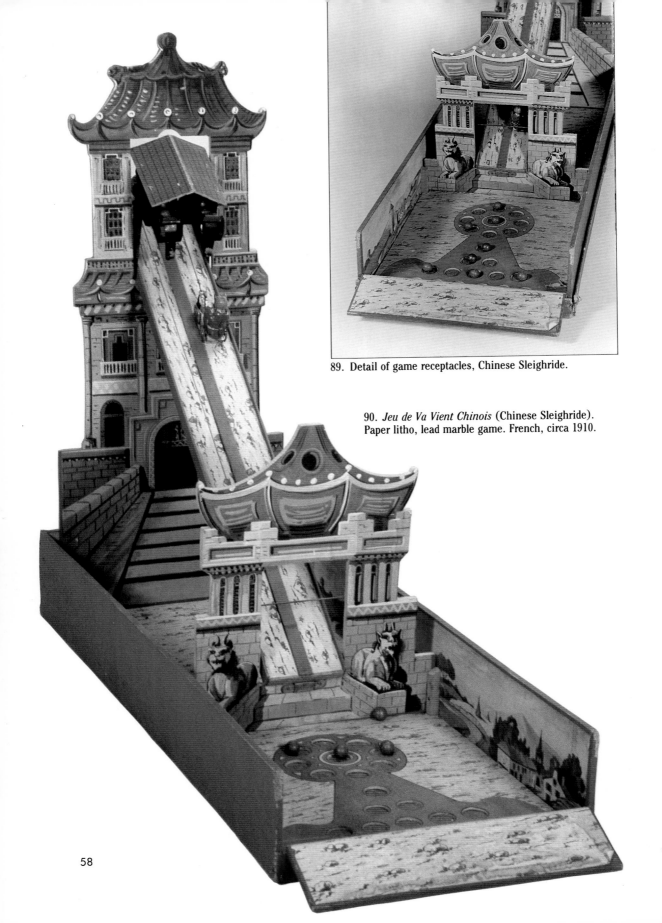

89. Detail of game receptacles, Chinese Sleighride.

90. *Jeu de Va Vient Chinois* (Chinese Sleighride).
Paper litho, lead marble game. French, circa 1910.

58

ever, we must mention a patent of 1867 by Kellis Horde for a mouth-operated, pneumatic mechanical bank. When air is blown by mouth through a tube, a crocodile is pushed forward to grab a penny in its jaws. Inhaling pulls the crocodile back and deposits the penny inside the bank. We do not know whether any of these are extant or if any were even manufactured, but it is the only pneumatic mechanical bank we have ever heard of.

Hand Power

Direct use of the hand is employed in complicated motions such as string-operated puppets (figure 96) and jumping jacks. In the latter, squeezing at one point produces a torque in the string loop that causes the jumping jack to somersault. An interesting direct hand-

91. Bubble blower. Cast iron, hand-operated bellows. James Walker, Birmingham, English, 1880.

92. Smoker. Hand-painted tin, clockwork with bellows. Gunthermann, German, circa 1890.

93. Chicken squeak toy. Wooden cage with bellows, spring-opened door. German, circa 1928.

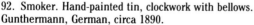

94. Lady at spinning wheel. Manivelle, hand-cranked automaton with music. European, circa 1870.

95. Mechanism of manivelle spinning wheel.

96. Dancers. Cloth dressed, on string spun platforms. French, circa 1900.

operated toy is the pecking bird toy, often made of wood, with a weight hanging below the birds on strings attached to them. As the hand swings the weight around and around, the birds peck in order.

The hand is used in beautiful animated music boxes of the last century called manivelles. In the manivelle, which means crank or crank handle in French, the careful, steady turning of a crank is power source and governor at the same time (figures 94, 95, and 100).

Spring Storage

The most versatile of all power sources in toys, until the ubiquitous battery of the recent present, is a spring of some kind. A spring may be made of anything that, when deformed, liberates the power by returning to its original configuration.

One of the simplest spring toys, not thought of as a spring, is a balloon which

97. Compression spring twirls airplanes. Einfalt (Kosmos), German, circa 1930.

98. Helical or barrel spring powering donkey cart. Lehmann NA-OB, German, patent 1903.

99. Spiral spring in an American clockwork mechanism.

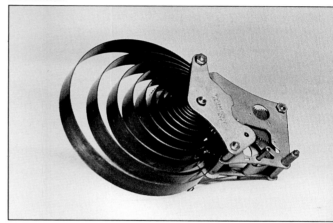

is blown up and, when released, expels its air through an orifice and jets all over the place. Here, the spring is the rubber of the balloon.

Rubber bands, so cheap and common, have been used in many toys, notably airplanes that actually fly. Rubber bands have also been used with devices to slow their unwinding to operate mechanical toys, particularly by French toymaker Fernand Martin. In a rubber band-powered boat, the propeller turning in the water slows the unwinding. In an unusual rowboat, the oars slow the unwinding.

The greatest use by far is of steel springs in spring toys called wind-ups to distinguish them from earlier, finer clockworks from which they all derived. The spring may be a flat band wound in a spiral, as in a clock spring (figure 99), or a spring wire wound in a helix. The helical spring may be used by twisting the ends in a wind-up, commonly called a barrel spring (figure 98). Occasionally, the helical spring is used as an extension spring simply pulling on a rack which turns a pinion, as in the coin-operated arcade device the Democratic Decision Maker (figures 29 and 30). Helical compression springs are very seldom used in toys as power storage (figure 97). One notable exception is a pair of biplanes made by Martin where a compression spring forces the planes up a helical wire causing them to fly around a pylon (figure 198).

100. Three dancers. Manivelle, Jumeau dolls with music. French, circa 1880.

Springs can be wound by the hand in different ways, generally by twisting a key but sometimes by depressing a lever which winds the spring (lever action wind-ups), and sometimes by actually winding by hand the wheel or other rotating part of the toy backward and then releasing it. In one ingenious mechanism, the winding key not only winds the spring but also carries driving wheels that steer the mechanism in cycloidal paths (figure 104).

Wind-up spring toys, the most versatile, are all derived from spring-driven clocks of the Middle Ages, and are called clockwork toys. Springs may never be used to propel full-scale vehicles in real

101. Amos 'n' Andy taxi. Tin litho, spring-driven. Marx, American, 1930s.

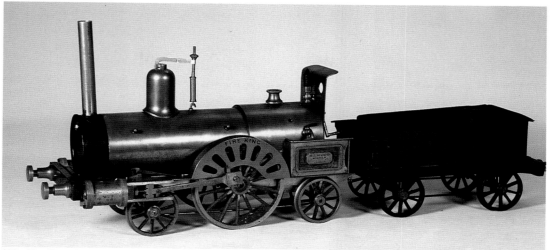

102. *Fire King.* Large-gauge steam locomotive, brass and steel with wooden coaches. H. J. Wood, London, English, circa 1860.

life, but they are the most common source of power in their tiny counterparts (figure 101).

Heat Engines

Heat engines is a general term for power sources that depend on the presence of a difference of temperature. The commonest are, of course, the wonderful toy steam engines (figure 103). In these heat engines, the power source is quite remote from the child's hand. Any fuel that burns creates a high temperature at one point in the steam engine; the difference between that and the ambient temperature in the room generates the power. In the simple steam engine, fuel is put under the water in a boiler. The steam thus generated creates pressure that oscillates a piston which, by means of a crank, turns a flywheel (figure 102). The fuel can be anything from fine nuggets of coal (rarely used) to alcohol or specially

prepared solid fuel pellets.

Many collectors love steam engines but don't run them very often because they must be cleaned afterward. Our preference is for hot-air engines where, instead of water and steam, the working fluid is simply air. All one need do is heat the bulb of the hot-air engine and the engine runs; remove the heat and it slows and stops (figure 106).

The difference between a hot-air engine and a steam engine is that, with steam, the pressure of the steam pushes a piston that, through a crank, turns the flywheel. In a hot-air engine, there are two cylinders. One cylinder moves the hot air into the other, the "working" cylinder, where the air cools, contracts, and sucks the piston back to work the flywheel.

An utterly simple but very interesting heat-powered toy is a little piece of bi-metal shaped like a disk, frog, or other

103. Frisbee steam engine. Cast iron and brass, hand-painted. American, circa 1870.

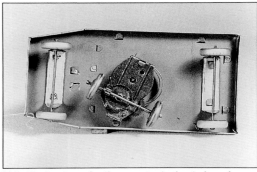

104. Mechanism of railway porter both winds and steers toy. U.S. Zone, West Germany, 1950s.

105. Electromagnet crank motor. Circa 1900.

animal held in the palm of the hand—which is the heat source. When placed on the table, the two dissimilar metals of the bimetal sheet contract differently as they cool and cause the toy to leap suddenly into the air.

Other heat engines on the exotic side depend on the difference between the wet bulb temperature on the beak of a toy drinking bird and the ambient temperature on the bird's bottom (figure 108). The bird oscillates back and forth, alternately dipping and raising its beak. When it dips its beak into a drinking vessel, this warms the top and forces a volatile liquid (freon, the same chemical that cools a refrigerator) inside the bird to the bottom, making it stand upright again. As water evaporates from the beak it cools the top, sucking the liquid to the top again. The process repeats over and over until the water in the drinking vessel is used up.

An exotic heat engine from the Space Age is a coil of wire with a memory, which loses its spring when hot and re-members its shape when cold. Dunk one end in your coffee and the wheels will turn. Another use of this memory wire is a boat in which you put an ice cube or two and the temperature difference between the ice and the water in which the boat floats propels it. These are intriguing new high-tech toys as are the tiny helicopters whose rotors are turned when the sun shines on a solar cell.

Electricity

Even before electric current was discovered in the early part of the nineteenth

106. *Russisches Karussell* [Russian carousel (ferris wheel)]. Doll, German, 1910.
Hot-air engine. Tin litho spirit burner. Bing, German, 1910.

107. Mechanism of battery-operated toy. Japanese, modern.

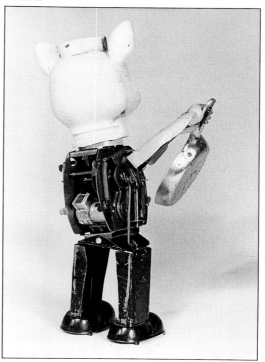

century, static electricity, the electricity that Benjamin Franklin experimented with using a kite, was used in toys. Small artificial lightning flashes could be made with machines where static electricity was generated by rubbing cat's fur over glass. Little paper figures were made to dance and rolling machines rotated by the coronal discharges off the tips of protruding wires, a reaction engine similar to Hero's but this time with static electricity discharges instead of discharges of steam. The originals of these esoteric static electric toys are hard to come by, although laboratory static generators can be obtained.

The first toy electric motors depended on magnetism, as all electric motors do. An electromagnet, substituted for the piston and cylinder of a steam engine,

108. Happy bird. Heat engine, glass and plastic. Taiwan, modern.

109. Magician. Hand-operated automaton. French, circa 1880.

alternately cranked a flywheel as the direct current was switched on and off by a breaker on a rotating shaft (figure 105).

Rotating motors with armatures working on batteries followed and later electric trains and other toys that could be plugged into house current. They almost always used transformers to bring the voltage down so as not to endanger children.

Now most toys operate with tiny electric motors (figure 107), so that the cost of keeping the toy in batteries is often more than that of the toy itself!

The Hand Alone

Any toy, spring-wound, steam-driven, or otherwise powered, can be operated and governed by hand alone. You can take out the spring and just turn the gearing by hand and watch the toy move. A steam accessory is a misnomer. It has a wheel that can be powered by a steam engine, an inertial flywheel, a spring motor, or, indeed, simply rotated by the finger. The finger of the hand then becomes both power and governor. The greatest examples are the manivelles which are turned and governed by hand, the pecking toys, or the magician which is worked by hand (figure 109) and displays the wonderful randomness that the human hand and brain communicate to it.

So although we have many power storage systems, we return to wonder at the human hand which releases and governs the release of the energy of sunshine through the food we eat stored in our bodies.

7 Governing Devices

110. Excelsior Sand Mill. Cast iron, hand-painted. American, circa 1890.

In toys directly operated by the hand where the hand itself is the power, the hand is also the governor and the hand-cranked toy can be operated faster or slower as one wishes. However, when energy is stored in a toy, mechanisms are necessary to govern its release so that the toy does not run too fast or too slow.

The governors in the early Greek singing birds—and temple doors —were controlled orifices through which air or water passed.

In toys where gravity provides the source of power, as in sand toys, small openings similar in function to the wasp waist of an

111. Marble escapement lets marbles drop one by one. Hand-painted tin. German, circa 1900.

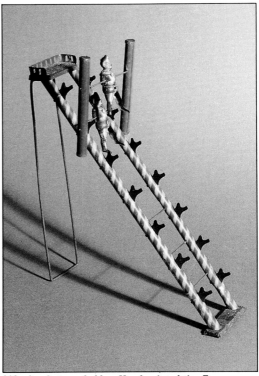

112. Acrobats on ladder. Hand-painted tin. European, circa 1910.

hourglass regulate the rate at which the sand trickles onto the wheel it turns, so that it does not dump all at once. In one cast-iron sand toy, a hopper over a wheel is turned by falling sand and a crank that activate a workman, making it appear that the man is operating the toy instead of the toy operating the man (figure 110). The simple mechanism is essentially the same as the one inside de Lauze's macabre toy of the French Revolution (figure 6). Many sand toys have been made over the course of several centuries, but the cheap ones made currently in the Orient work on exactly the same principle.

Escapements and Friction Governors

Where marbles are used as the source of power, they must be released one at a time by what might be called a crude escapement (figure 111).

Another use of an escapement is where the pallet descends a linear ratchet, as in a pair of acrobats on a ladder (figure 112). Fine lead shot moves in the tubes, causing the tumblers to leap over one another.

A very ancient and not very accurate clock escapement was the thread-and-weight escapement. As the mechanism revolved, a string wound around a wire, holding and then releasing the string to go on to another wire and so on, around and around (figure 113).

Many types of simple governors depend on friction to slow down the motion. The friction may be friction with the air (figure 114), as in a fly fan. Or the rotating part of the toy itself and its friction through the air may be used to govern the speed, such as in a carousel. In the simplest, a flying airplane, the friction of the whirling propeller in the air acts as both propeller and governor.

Water Resistance

Friction with water may also be a governor. The simplest case is a propeller or side-wheel driven boat (figure 115), where the friction is that of the water on the propeller itself or on the side-wheel.

In toy boats and swimming fish that were intended to be used in the water, the resistance of the water itself governs the speed.

To use friction as a governor, it is fundamental that, if the speed increases, the friction must increase to slow it down. Similarly, if the speed decreases, the friction must decrease to allow it to speed up, thus allowing the object to proceed at a steady rate. Resistance to air or water increases with speed—actually with the square of the speed—so that fly fans and propellers automatically govern to a steady rate.

One interesting use of water as a governor is in a toy whose clockwork causes a swan to swim around and around in a moat (figure 116). Water friction on the underside of the swan makes a wonderfully long-running governor; the largest

113. Thread-and-weight escapement. Tin litho, wind-up. Japanese, circa 1930.

114. Fly fan governing clockwork.

115. Warship with ramming bow. Painted metal, clockwork. Bing, German, circa 1912.

116. Swan in moat. Hand-painted tin with castle and zeppelin. German, circa 1920.

version will run for about twelve hours.

An interesting use of water as a governor is, of course, in swimming toys. Toys representing swimming fish or frogs preceded toys that represented humans swimming. Until the latter part of the nineteenth century, Europeans feared aquatic activity, believing that epidemics were caused by bathing outdoors.

The earliest swimming stroke was the breaststroke and the first swimming toys performed this stroke. A toy called Ondine, invented in 1876 (figure 118), was produced in at least three sizes by Charles Bertran and Elie Martin in Paris.[15] With a cork body, bisque head, and clockwork protected by an almost water-

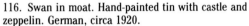

117. Swimmer Annette Kellermann. Hand-painted tin, fine clockwork with fly fan governor. Probably German, 1906.

proof brass case, Ondine demonstrated the breaststroke and could also swim on its back. Later versions, with a celluloid head, were mass-produced as late as 1929.

The breaststroke, backstroke, and sidestroke were the only recognized swimming maneuvers until the double overarm was introduced in 1893 by an Englishman, J. Trudgen, who learned it in South America. Finally, in 1896, swimming was accepted as an Olympic event.

In 1905, an Australian, Annette Kellermann, attempted to swim the English Channel, the first woman to do so. Although she did not succeed, she pioneered the use of the stroke called the Australian crawl, and even more daringly invented the one-piece swimsuit. It is not surprising that the first toy with an overarm swimmer, in a blue tank suit and red bathing cap (figure 117), appeared in 1906 celebrating her valiant effort. Kellermann not only revolutionized swimming

118. Ondine, two versions. *Swimmer on right* by Elie Martin, Paris, French, 1885; *on left,* mass-produced version by same firm, French, 1929.

119. Swimmers. *Top:* Annette Kellermann; *left and right:* two versions of Ondine; *foreground:* prewar Japanese celluloid swimming doll.

120. Carousel. Hand-painted tin and cloth. Althof Bergmann, American, circa 1870.

but also made it possible to simplify the mechanism of swimming toys. Later Japanese celluloid swimmers appeared, using the overarm stroke (figure 119).

Air Resistance

Other types of governors employ air resistance or the rotation of the toy itself to control the rate of energy release. An Althof Bergmann carousel of 1870 (figure 120) is rotated smoothly by clockwork governed by the air resistance of the hand-painted tin gondolas and horses themselves which act as a fly fan. The overworked girl apparently turning the carousel by hand is cranked by the clockwork hidden in the base.

In toy boats and airplanes, the propeller has a dual function. It provides forward thrust and acts as a fly fan governor to control the rate of energy released from the spring or, in some cases, the rubber band. While a fly fan is a governor, an equally fast spinning heavy flywheel is not, the difference being that the fly fan is designed to have great air resistance and the flywheel is smooth and has very little.

Solid Friction

For vehicles and figures that move on wheels, the friction created as the toy travels over a surface is often an adequate governor.

Friction of solid against solid can also be a governor. The most elementary situation is one where clockwork drives the wheels of a traveling toy with no governor at all. The friction of the wheels rolling over the surface is in itself a governor. You can prove this to yourself by taking one of these toys, running it on a smooth tabletop, and then trying to run it on the carpet. It will run much faster on the table where the wheel-to-surface friction is less.

The best solid-to-solid friction governors embody the principle that the friction increases as the toy speeds up and decreases as it slows down. This is accomplished by little weights which are flung outward by centrifugal force. When the speed increases too much, they rub on a surface and slow it down. These are the centrifugal governors used in phonographs and wind-up toy trains (figures 121 and 122).

One can also use magnetism as a governor, but we know of no toy in which this is employed.

In real life, when we want to reduce speed we reduce power. If you want to go more slowly in your automobile, you take your foot off the accelerator. Less gasoline reaches the motor, power is re-

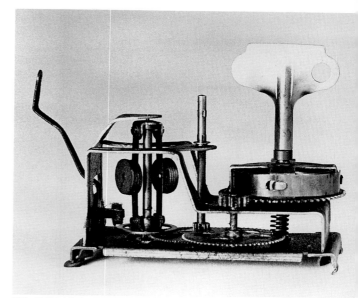

121. Solid-friction centrifugal governor of Bing Pigmyphone.

122. Centrifugal solid-friction train governor, *on left* behind driving wheels.

duced, and the air friction around the car and the friction of the tires against the road slow down the speed. In toy steam engines, very few have centrifugally operated governors that cut down the flow of steam to the cylinder. Mostly, the regulation of a steam engine is done by adjusting the steam flow by hand. In hot-air engines, we can move the heat closer or farther away to increase or decrease speed. In electrically driven toys, such as electric railroads, we cut the power by means of a rheostat which decreases the electrical power going to the motor.

Pendulums and Escapements
We have left the governing of spring-actuated toys to the end of this chapter

123. Camel nodder. Papier-mâché and cloth, clockwork. European, circa 1900.

124. Pecking bird. Hand-painted, clockwork. German, circa 1910.

even though these are the most common of old toys, the clockwork toys and nodders.

A fundamental governor in many toys is the pendulum. It may be used vertically, as in a clock, or horizontally, as in a nodder (figure 123). Or it may be inverted so that the pivot point is at the bottom, as in many wind-up walkers.

As this whole class of toys, clockwork and wind-ups, derive from a common ancestor, the pendulum clock, it is most interesting to start with the most fundamental type. Because the head rocks or an arm beckons (figure 124), they are called nodders. Nodders were probably made before clockwork, notably in Japan, and so delicately balanced were the heads and arms that they kept in motion from natural air currents and vibrations in the room. Many recent nodders are made without any clockwork. Balancing figures that balance upright (figure 125) work on exactly the same principle: they are just compound pendulums.

Clockwork nodders are really simple clocks without dials. A large tiger (figure 126) nods its head for over an hour, beating almost perfect second intervals. For a clock pendulum to beat seconds, the pendulum must be about a yard long. The nodder, however, uses a horizontal compound pendulum with the head as the weight at one end, a counterweight inside the body at the other end, and a pivot at the neck. It is actuated by an ordinary clock escapement. Most interesting is that the jaw of the tiger is a tiny compound pendulum with the same pe-

125. Monkey balancer. Tin litho on wooden perch. American, circa 1930.

126. Nodding tiger, clockwork with escapement. Papier-mâché and fabric. Probably German, circa 1900.

127. Man driving donkey wind-up. Tin litho cart with hand-painted figures. Gunthermann, German, circa 1910.

128. Clockwork mechanism of Gunthermann donkey cart, showing eccentric weight governor.

riod (one second) as the head, so that as the head nods the mouth opens and closes in resonance.

Any pendulum-governed mechanism has an escapement. This is composed of a ratchet wheel, not unlike a gear wheel, with what is called a pallet. The pallet oscillates back and forth to allow only one tooth at a time to advance.

Clockwork toys are actually only those in which the power stored in the spring is governed by escapements invented for clocks. Yet the term *clockwork* has often been used inaccurately to refer to all spring-driven toys.

The difference between clockwork in clocks and clockwork in music boxes and automata is simply that the pendulum in clocks makes the mechanism turn very slowly. For music boxes and toys, it is desirable to have the mechanism turn quickly; therefore the pendulum governor is replaced by a fly fan. We have often taken a good old clockwork, removed the escapement, and put metal blades on the fastest-running wheel, thus controlling the speed.

Clockwork escapements allow one tooth at a time to escape from a pallet at regular intervals in order to keep springs from springing. The pallet rocks back and forth, governed by a pendulum or an oscillating piece as in a watch escapement. In another form of governor, instead of an oscillating piece, there is an eccentric, fast-moving small weight that acts as the governor. This is akin to a pendulum (figures 127 and 128).

In the later, cheaper wind-up movements, the pallet itself constituted the rapidly clicking pendulum. In some escapements, the toy itself acts as the oscillating pendulum. This is characteristic of many walking figure toys.

A delicate mechanical horse (figure 129), rocked by the motion of an inverted conical pendulum, is as elegant in the simplicity of its mechanism as in the grace of its design. The clockwork in the body of the horse rotates a bent shaft that protrudes from the horse's back into the rider. As the horsewoman's weight shifts from pommel to cantle, her mount rocks in harmonic resonance.

The origin of this toy has always been something of a mystery to us. The horse is hand-carved wood and the bisque-headed rider carries a crop crowned by a fox. Although the style appears French, the French rarely worked in wood and they never hunted foxes. After correctly deciding it must be English, we leaped to the conclusion that it was Victorian. It was not until this book was in

129. Clockwork horsewoman. Velvet-dressed figure on wooden rocking horse. English, modern.

galleys that it was pointed out to us that it is clearly signed "W. Summerbell" on the bottom of the rockers' crosspiece and was made in limited quantities in England in the 1970s. Whether or not it is a reproduction of an earlier piece we do not know. In any case, it is an ingenious application of the inverted conical pendulum.

Cheap, mass-produced wind-up toys were not in any sense "clock" works. They were springs with gears and generally a rather crude oscillating pallet for a governor.

To regulate a pendulum clock or a pendulum toy, wind it and listen. Perhaps it says *tock tick*. If it does, tilt it until it goes *tick tock* and then tilt it less until it goes *tick tick*.

8 Mechanisms That Provide Action

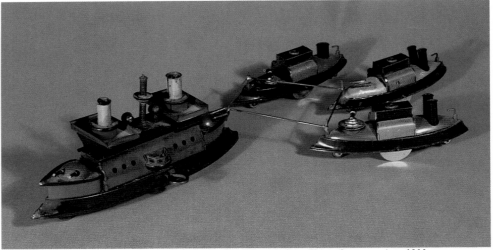

130. Flotilla, dreadnought towing torpedo boats. Tin litho wind-up. Hess, German, circa 1910.

The third component of a mechanical toy, after the power source and the governor—and perhaps the most important—is the mechanism. Here the ingenuity of the toy maker comes to full flower. The devices employed to transform motion from one form to another, such as rotation to oscillation, run the whole gamut of mechanisms, intricate in concept and simple in execution. Essentially, no familiar schemes were overlooked and many new ones were invented. Indeed, so many and various are the ingenious mechanisms that we can hope to introduce only some basic ones.

131. Equestrienne. Flywheel-powered. W. Britain & Sons, English, circa 1890.

132. Stevedore. Tin litho wind-up. Wuco, West German, 1950s.

Wheels

Starting with the simplest components of mechanisms, we must mention the wheel. Pull toys roll on wheels running freely. Toys with power are driven along by the turning of the wheels.

To give action to the toy, the wheels sometimes are eccentric; that is, the axle is not in the center of the wheel but displaced. Eccentric wheels can cause toy ships to roll and pitch. The Hess flotilla (figure 130) consists of a wind-up battleship with an eccentric wheel towing three torpedo boats. As the battleship pitches up and down, the wire between it and the torpedo boats also moves up and down, causing them to appear to be buffeted by waves.

133. Stevedore in action.

134. Tightrope cyclist. Cloth-dressed composition figure on cast-iron bicycle. Circa 1920.

Eccentric wheels can also cause miniature horses to gallop. W. Britain & Sons, London toy manufacturers who began business in the 1880s, combined flywheel power with eccentric wheels in several very successful toys. The Equestrienne, circa 1890, is powered by the momentum of a rapidly spinning flywheel spun by hand (figure 131). The conical end of the flywheel axle rides as a bevel pinion around the outside of a circular base to rotate the assembly of flywheel, horse, and rider. A horizontal cam in the base causes the tutu-clad rider to leap over a bar and regain her seat on her steed. The horse, in turn, is given a galloping motion by an eccentric wheel between its hind legs.

Another, most interesting "wheel" is a

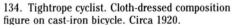

cube that rolls—a square wheel if you like. In a toy made in West Germany after World War II (figures 132 and 133), the wind-up is in a square crate. As the crate tumbles along, the camlike action of its shape moves a stevedore as though he were pushing and tumbling it.

Levers and Cranks

Other fundamental components are levers of all different kinds which, used in connection with a crank on a wheel or gear wheel, transform the rotary motion to an up-and-down or back-and-forth motion. There are numerous applications of this mechanism. An ingenious Japanese circus toy has a wind-up in the back. A rotating crank lifts a wire up and down, causing a tightrope walker to slide back and forth on the wire.

Cranks are also used to transform linear push-pull motion into rotary motion, the way the piston of a steam engine pushes and pulls the crank that turns the flywheel. Familiar to everyone is the reciprocating motion of the pistons and connecting rods on the driving wheels of steam locomotives, both in the toy world and in the real one.

While cranks give a repetitive motion with each turn of the wheel, cams, which are wheels with specially shaped irregular edges, can be used to produce a series of different motions to a lever. These are frequently resorted to, especially in elaborate combination in princely automata (figure 141) and in slightly less complicated form by the Vielmetter and JWB artists (figure 26).

135. Clown on unicycle. Hand-painted tin string toy, lead wheel and counterbalance. Probably French, circa 1900.

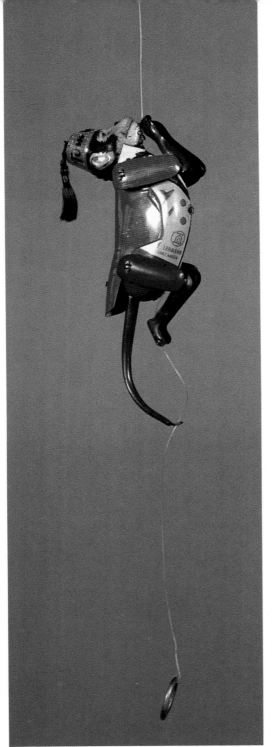

137. Climbing monkey. Cardboard. The Dolly Toy Company, American, probably 1940s.

Strings and Pulleys

A mechanism used to actuate many toys is a simple string (figure 135). A tight-rope cyclist on a bicycle (figure 134), balanced on a string by a heavy weight below, appears to pedal backward and forward as one end of the string is raised and lowered. The mechanism, in this case the bicycle, moves the figure's legs in a realistic manner. Here again, instead of the person working the machine, the machine works the person, as if to remind us not to submit to the tyranny of the machine in real life.

Various climbing toys—monkeys on

136. Tom the Climbing Monkey. Tin litho. Lehmann #888, Germany, manufactured 1953–1970. Older version, #385, made 1895–1945, differs only in that the jacket is rough-sprayed.

strings, sailors on ropes, and ascending balloons, for example—depend on simple differential pulleys where the string that is pulled from below wraps around a smaller pulley rotating a larger one on the same axle. When the string is pulled down the toy goes up, and when the string is released the toy comes down by gravity. Tom the Climbing Monkey (figure 136), manufactured in Germany by Lehmann from 1895 to 1945 (EPL #385) and again from 1953 to 1970 (EPL #888),[16] used a mechanism akin to the ancient Chinese windlass. Two pulleys of different sizes give a mechanical advantage for lifting weights, identical to the mechanism used in hand chain hoists in real life. With the upside-down engineering of the toy maker, the pull of the hand replaces the weight and raises the windlass—in this case, the monkey. There is a cardboard version (figure 137), probably made during wartime shortages of metal. Here, as in most toys, the energy is ingeniously applied backward.

There are toy zeppelins where the string upon which the zeppelin hangs passes through the body of the zeppelin, wraps around the shaft of the propeller, and, as gravity causes the zeppelin to descend, the string turns the propeller (figure 138).

Endless Chains

Endless belts, strings, or chains, winding around pulleys, cause figures and vehicles to move along a predetermined path. In a manivelle of Hamburg Harbor (figure 139), an endless cloth belt moves

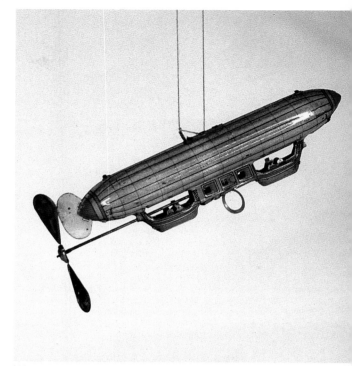

138. Zeppelin. Tin litho, string operated. Probably German, 1920s.

139. Hamburg Harbor manivelle. Paper litho on cardboard. German, circa 1910.

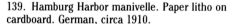

140. Dining monkeys automaton. Cast-metal heads, redressed, electric motor replaces original clockwork. Possibly Decamps, French, circa 1900.

141. Mechanism of dining monkeys automaton.

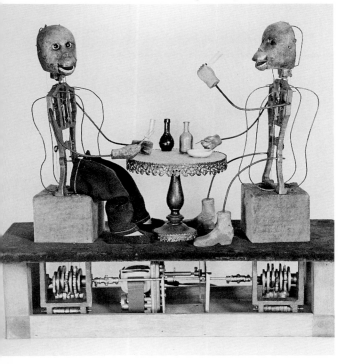

142. Pea eater. Lithographed tin, wind-up. German, illustrated in catalogue of Moses Kohnstam (Moko), Nürnberg, 1928–30.

boats across the scene to disappear at one end and reappear at the other. Figure 8 showed a company of Zouaves with mounted officers, a band, and cannon parading in review before Napoleon III to the accompaniment of martial music from a fine music box in a toy that must date back to about 1860. The soldiers, horses, and cannon are drawn in formation by an endless chain following an intricate path around five sprocket wheels.

A different kind of endless chain is the ancient mechanism of eaters and drinkers. A marvelous mechanism is the one of a drinker who pours from a bottle, drinks from the glass, then pours from the bottle again, ad infinitum. The secret of this mechanism is simply that the glass in the drinker's left hand is connected by a tube to the bottle in his right hand, and when he lifts the glass to enjoy his drink, the liquid drains back into the bottle so that he can pour again (figures 143 and 144).

Eaters are also intriguing. A great one is the German pea eater who kicks a pea into the air from his top hat (figure 142). The pea lands in his mouth. Again, like the drinker, the pea completes the circuit by rolling down through a channel in the

figure's arm and returns to the top hat.

Simulated drinking and eating are portrayed in an automaton in which two monkeys seated at a table perform a series of seven complicated motions controlled by fourteen brass cams in the base. Each in turn lifts a spoon or fork, opens its mouth, chews and chatters, turns its head, opens and closes both eyes, toasts the other, and winks (figures 140 and 141).

143. Drinking bear. Brass bottle and cup, real fur. Decamps, French, circa 1880.

144. Mechanism of drinking bear, showing how liquid drains through tube from cup to bottle.

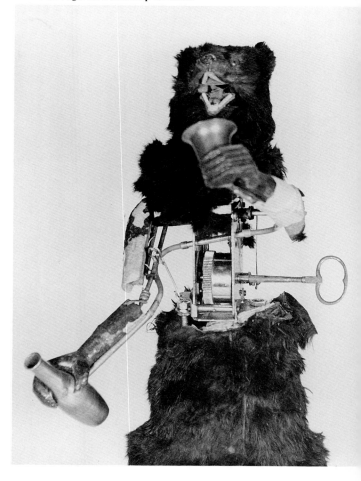

Out-of-Balance on Purpose

An out-of-balance flywheel that rotates freely can cause toy animal and human figures to jiggle around and birds to peck. The mounted cowboy's twirling lariat jerks his horse in circles (figure 145). In 1938, Ferdinand Strauss, an American toy maker, marketed an ingeniously simple mechanism in the brightly lithographed tinplate Ferdinand the Bull (figure 148), based on a beloved children's book. In this version of the bull who would rather smell the flowers than fight the toreadors, Ferdinand's tail is an out-of-balance flywheel. As the tail swings downward on each rotation, the back feet are lifted slightly and the hindquarters are free to move in reaction to the tail's rotation. Thus Ferdinand, while unsuccessfully trying to dislodge a bumblebee on his rump, stomps around the tabletop with a brightly colored flower clamped firmly in his teeth.

In real life, for smooth-running machinery, an out-of-balance flywheel would be anathema. It would shake the useful device to pieces. If your automobile wheels are out of balance, your tires soon become useless. In a toy, out-of-balance is a joy and shakes us with laughter.

Walking Toys

Although the inverted pendulum is the most widely used principle for mechanical walkers and rockers, other toys are

146. Walking Uncle Tom. Cloth-dressed cast-iron figure, clockwork. Ives, American, circa 1890.

147. Walking Uncle Tom's one-way shoes.

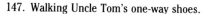

145. Cowboy with lariat. Tin litho, wind-up. Marx, American, 1930s.

148. Ferdinand the Bull. Tin litho, wind-up. Strauss, American, 1930s.

149. Woman with four legs pulling cart. Hand-painted tin, flywheel-powered. German, circa 1890.

150. Mechanism of cockfight.

made to walk with one-way shoes that slide forward but not backward (figures 146 and 147). In one fairly modern toy with one-way shoes for horses, the whole track jiggles back and forth to move the horses forward as they race toward the finish line. From the viewpoint of mechanisms, one-way shoes are a ratchet. A ratchet slides one way without difficulty and grips when the pull is in the other direction.

The first American patent (Number 33,019, August 6, 1861) that relates to walking appears to be a toy motor to work feet invented by E. R. Morrison. Clockwork lifts each foot alternately as the other foot pushes it forward. In the following year, 1862, E. R. Morrison patented the autoperipatetikos walking

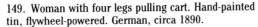

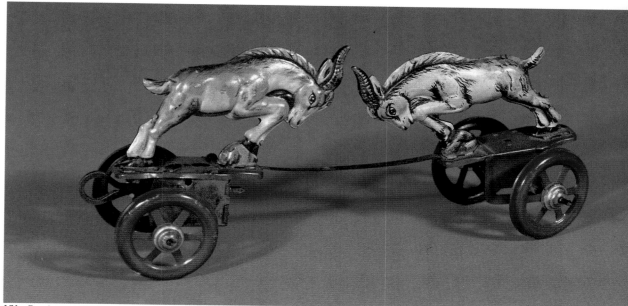

151. Butting goats. Tin litho. Gebr. Einfalt (Kosmos), German, circa 1928.

152. Cockfight. Tin litho wind-up. Gebr. Einfalt (Kosmos), German, circa 1928.

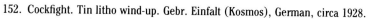

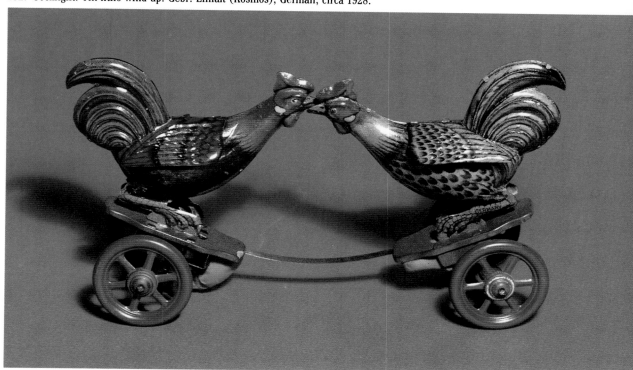

153. Birds fighting for a worm. Hand-painted tin. German, circa 1905.

154. Airplane descending helical wire. Tin, wood, and wire with celluloid propeller. German, circa 1910.

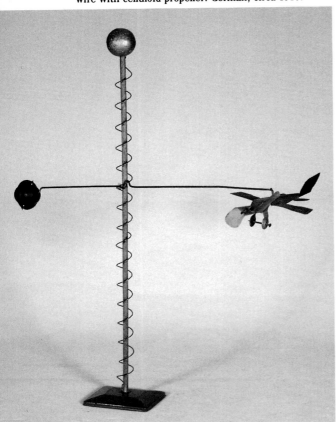

doll powered by his motor (figure 37).

Another way of showing walking in a toy is by what one might call optical illusion. A German tin toy (figure 149) has a woman who, in reality, has four legs which as she moves along simply rotate like a four-spoked wheel without a rim.

Reversing Mechanisms

Many toys use sudden reversals of motion to achieve comic effects. The resulting inertial shocks provide the action in such toys as those in which two cocks fight (figure 152), a steamroller moves back and forth, or a donkey-pulled cart jerks so as to cause the donkey to buck and kick.

In the cockfight, the reversing is accomplished by a half-crown wheel that alternately engages a pinion on one wheel and, after half a revolution, turns the other wheel in the opposite direction (figure 150). A flat spring connecting the combatants absorbs the inertial shock by

155. Mechanism of shunting locomotive "112." Tin litho. Orbro, German, circa 1910.

bending and straightening, giving the lithographed tinplate birds a fierce, life-like dodging-and-pecking action. This mechanism can be found in many different applications involving two figures, such as goats butting (figure 151) or a toreador striking at a plunging bull.

The earlier version of these toys had two birds fighting for a worm (figure 153). Instead of a flat spring, a helical spring representing the worm itself was used. Each bird has one end of the worm firmly clamped in its beak.

Among the reversing mechanisms is a crank with a toothed rack that is moved back and forth to rotate a pinion, causing the wheels of a shunting locomotive to turn one way and then the other (figure 155).

Archimedes Screw

The Archimedes screw of antiquity is frequently used to cause clockwork rotation which lifts balls to the top of inclines and allows them to roll down freely. Archimedes (287–212 B.C.) devised this screw for removing water from the hold of a ship. In one Japanese toy produced before World War II (figures 156 and 157), a celluloid ball coasts down an intricate ramp and is then lifted to its starting point by an Archimedes screw

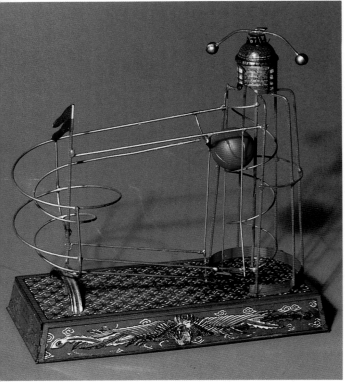

156. Rolling ball raised by Archimedes screw. Tin litho wind-up. Japanese, circa 1930.

157. Detail of verge escapement on Archimedes screw toy.

powered by clockwork in the base. A simple escapement at the top of the tower adds movement while serving as a governor. These are the antecedents of the screw feeds that lift grain into silos on modern farms.

In another helical wire toy, a wind-up airplane flies itself and its counterweight to the top of the helical wire, where the airplane turns around and circles down again by gravity.

The Archimedes screw works in reverse on some very simple, clever toys. In one aerial toy (figure 154), a bar from which an airplane and its counterweight are suspended is placed at the top of an Archimedes screw and rotates as gravity pulls it downward, causing the airplane to fly around and around. This system is analogous to a bolt with very stretched-out threads pointing upward. When the nut is placed on top, the weight of the nut rotates it and screws it down. In real life, we do not want the pressure on nuts to unscrew them; therefore threads are quite fine and close together.

9

Sounds and

158. *Mikasa.* Tin litho warship, clockwork. Bing, German, circa 1910.

Other Surprises

In some exciting toys, a trigger provides a surprise ending. In real life, triggers are used in guns; their purpose, just the opposite of a governor's, is to release pent-up energy all at once. This is just what triggers do in toys. Perhaps the oldest and best known is the jack-in-the-box, which is pressed down against a spring. The lid of the box is then closed and secured. When the hook (trigger) is released, up jack jumps.

A torpedo fired at a ship made by Schoenhut unexpectedly blows it to bits (figures 159 and 161). An earlier Ives locomotive travels

159. Submarine and Dreadnought Naval War Toy. Wood with spring triggers. Schoenhut, American, pat. April 6, 1915.

160. Typical clockwork boat mechanism.

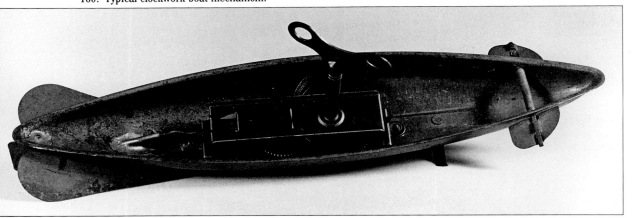

along and then suddenly disintegrates. These toys can be put together again in anticipation of another disaster. The life-size Decamps chicken walks along sedately until she has the urge to drop an egg. A Schoenhut ski jumper schusses down a snow-covered ramp and throws himself over a high jump, propelled by a hidden trigger in the ramp. Our ski jumper once leaped so high that he landed on the floor and broke his leg.

One of the most interesting surprise toys is a Bing clockwork boat called *Mikasa* (figure 158). Boats, like trains, are very difficult to play with. Trains need a lot of space; boats need water, which rusts toys and makes a mess. Boats are usually simple-minded; they are just driven through the water (figure 160). *Mikasa* is different; she has an ingenious mechanism and a surprise ending. You wind her up and set two triggers, inserting caps such as those used in cap pistols behind the two naval guns mounted on the deck. Before running the boat, both triggers are cocked. *Mikasa* then propels herself away and fires her first gun, which engages the rudder mechanism, putting her into a 180-degree turn. The second gun then fires and kicks the rudder so that the boat straightens out and heads back in the direction from which she came.

As in the case of Fernand Martin's Madelon who drops the plates and the Ives locomotive which disintegrates, *Mikasa*'s triggers are activated by the expansion of the mainspring so that the action comes toward the end of a long run and causes the surprise.

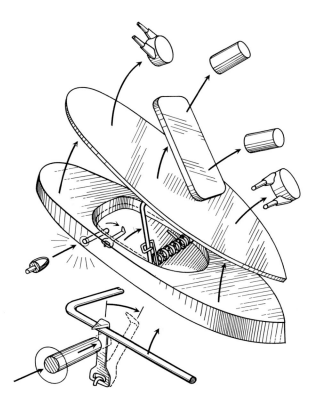

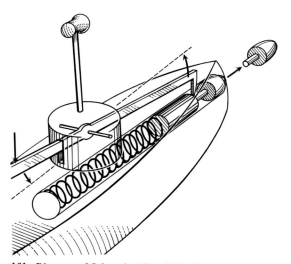

161. Diagram of Schoenhut Naval War Toy.

162. Nürnberg dancers. Celluloid and iron.
J. Schoenner, German, circa 1920.

163. Reading bear. Cloth-dressed tin litho, wind-up.
Japanese, 1950s.

Magnetic Magic

Following experiments with magnetism at Dublin University in 1838, a flurry of magnetically operated toys resulted.[17] The Nürnberg figures from the famous toy-making center in Germany make use of magnetism. The vertical axis of a spinning flywheel that protrudes from the center of the dance floor is a permanent magnet (figure 162). Different iron shapes on the feet of the figures are attracted to the magnet, the rotation of which causes them to perform appropriate motions. There is a triangular base for three-step waltzers, a kidney shape for a gliding skater, and a hollow circle enabling a clown to chase a pig.

A phonograph toy of about the same era as the spindle-driven pugilists, cocks, and political figures (figure 35) differs in that it depends on a magnetic axle powered by the edge of the phonograph record to achieve its action (figure 164). Instead of being inertially powered by a spinning flywheel, the ballroom dancers are powered by the rotation of the phonograph records. The phonograph version adds the dimension of music; it is fun to see the couple dance to a foxtrot or polka of the 1920s.

In a magical book, the professor's hand may be placed on any of several questions. When the book is closed, magnetism operates so that when the book is opened again the figure opposite the professor is pointing to the answer. A much more modern bear (figure 163) quickly flips the metal pages of a book with a tiny magnet in his hand. He is, indeed, a speed reader.

Randomness and Games of Chance

Randomness, necessary to make the action of a toy unpredictable, is the most difficult thing to achieve in a mechanical device. In the real world, randomness is achieved by the drawings in state lotteries and, slightly controlled, in gambling casinos by the use of cards, dice, and roulette wheels. Slot machines are mechanical devices that have a reasonably random outcome. This quality is sought to introduce the element of chance in a variety of toys.

Old French horse race games (figure 166) simply spun a number of horses by a lever-wound tension-spring mechanism governed by friction. The horses whizzed around a racetrack and, much like a roulette wheel, the one with its

164. The Magnetic Dancers. Tin litho. National Co., American, patented August 1922.

165. Gee-Wiz horse race. Tin litho, string-spun flywheel. Wolverine, American, 1923.

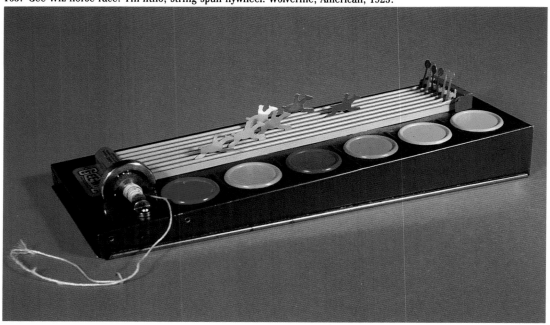

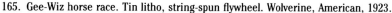

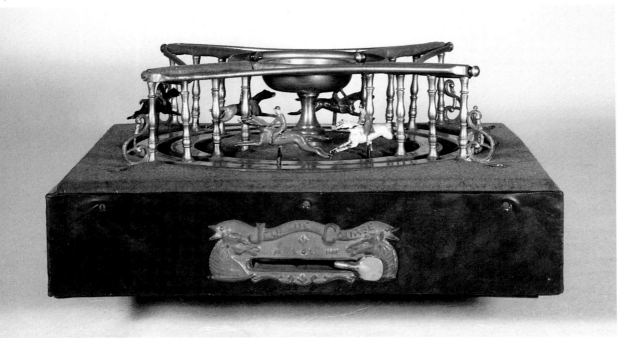

166. Horse race. Cast-metal horses on baize-covered wooden box. French, circa 1910.

167. Jouster. Hand-painted tin wind-up. European, circa 1910.

nose closest to the finish won—a not very realistic race.

In a far more successful effort, toy horses leap forward when they are hit by steel balls. The balls have been randomly struck by a rapidly spinning square arbor rotated by the inertia of a flywheel spun by pulling a string. The balls roll down an incline to be shot up again.

This system comes in toy form, about a foot long with six horses, made as the Gee-Wiz by Wolverine in both England and the United States (figure 165). Wolverine also made an elaborate large version with eight horses that works on house current and probably was a real gambling machine.

A more elegant random device is a hand-painted tinplate jouster, made in Europe about 1880 (figure 167), who tilts at a ring as his horse trots around a course. An eccentric crank on the wheel under his mount causes him to post and his lance misses the ring more often than not.

Any toy operated by marbles can be arranged to receive marbles in different numbered pockets and usually is a gaming device. An interesting gambling toy is the French Le Zanzinet (figure 168), where dice are rolled and pieces of a pig are won according to the numbers shown on the dice. The effect is as random as the roll of the dice. Such nonrepetitive devices bridge the gap between mechanical toys and games of chance.

Noise, Sound, and Music

The simplest toy is a noisemaker. Some of us just enjoy plain noise.

Little toys that are simply inverted to say *moo* or *meow* or *mama* are cylinders where a weight depresses a paper bellows and expels air through an appropriately designed reed (figure 169). These can also be operated by having a spring and depressing the bellows by hand or, in the case of a caged bird, by a spring which opens the door and makes the noise simultaneously.

Any mechanical toy can be enhanced by the addition of sound. Probably the simplest and most effective mechanism is a small spring that clicks as it rubs over one of the gear wheels in the mechanism. This was used by Decamps to make his lions roar. Alternately, the

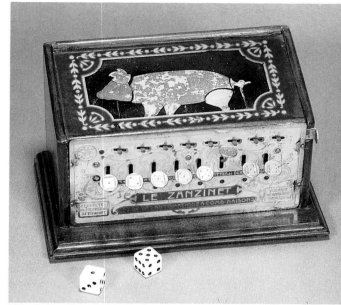

168. *Le Zanzinet: Jeu de des Automatique à Combinaisons.* Embossed brass and heavy metal in wood-and-glass box. M.F.I.N., Paris, French, circa 1890.

169. Cow moos when tail is depressed. Tin litho with bellows. American, 1920s.

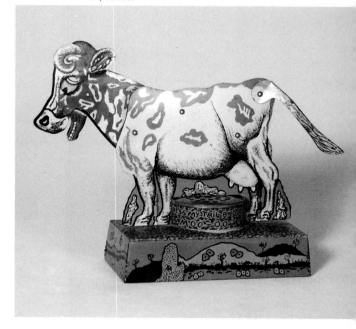

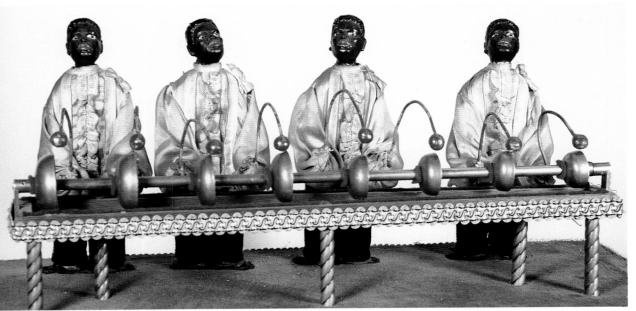

170. Bell-ringer automaton. A full octave of bells rings the changes. European, mid-1800s.

171. Mechanism of bell-ringer automaton. Fine brass clockwork, wooden spiked-barrel music box operating hammers.

mechanism can operate a bellows to make a squeak. The simplest dolls say *mama* when the body is pressed.

In hand-painted German tin toys called plinkety-plinks, a simple tune of about seven notes was used (figure 172). Earlier toys had much more complicated music boxes and figures, particularly automata (figures 170 and 171).

Speech

Edison made a talking doll with a tiny phonograph hidden in its body. A miniature version of the Edison phonograph (figure 173) was enclosed in the metal body of a doll, which had a German bisque head.

172. Clown with accordion. Cloth-dressed, hand-painted tin, wind-up plinkety-plink. Gunthermann, German, circa 1900.

173. Mechanism of Edison's phonograph doll. Edison Phonograph Toy Manufacturing Co., American, 1889.

There were attempts to synthesize speech, however, over a century before Edison recorded and reproduced the human voice. One must clearly distinguish between synthetic speech and the recording of actual speech, which was Edison's great contribution. Synthetic speech is like a painting; recorded speech is akin to a photograph. The earliest documented efforts to synthesize human speech took place around 1770 and were made by Friedrich von Knauss, Abbé Mical (Kratzenstein) of France, and von Kempelen (1778). These were the first attempts in a very simple way to synthesize speech with a machine, a problem that Archimedes had considered insoluble. The Kratzenstein device successfully reproduced the vowels *a, e, i, o,* and *u* by expelling air from bellows into tubes of different shapes. The machine won a prize at the St. Petersburg Imperial Academy of Science in 1779. Von Kempelen succeeded in synthesizing whole words such as *opera, astronomy,* and *Constantinopolis.*[18]

The first doll that said *mama* and *papa* was patented in 1823.

There is no question that here toys and automata preceded, although in a crude form, the use of synthetic speech, electronically contrived and perhaps first exhibited to the public by Bell Telephone at the World's Fair in New York in 1939 under the name Vocoder. Now, with the aid of computers, synthetic speech is possible but still difficult to accomplish.

A most beautiful toy that demonstrates synthetic speech is the Speaking Picture Book (figure 174), made in Germany in

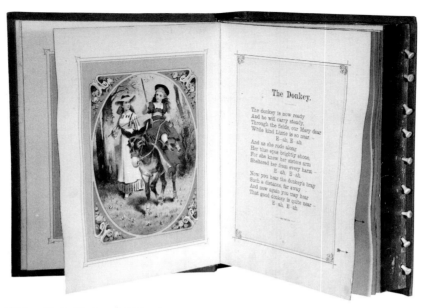

174. Speaking Picture Book. Illustrated children's book of verses with noise-making mechanisms inside. German, 1895.

1895. The mechanism, which produces nine different animal sounds, consists of seven bellows with complicated flute pipes with stops reminiscent of the shapes of the Kratzenstein pipes (figure 175). When the cover is opened, one reads a verse about a cow, sees a picture of it, and follows an arrow pointing to a string. When the string is pulled, a realistic *moo* sounds out. The verses were published in five languages, the pictures and sounds remaining the same.

Apart from the automata, the dolls that said *mama* and *papa,* and the cows that said *moo,* this Victorian toy, primitive though it is, is probably still the best synthetic speech toy to reach the market, and was certainly the predecessor of the Vocoder and of modern electronic voice synthesizers.

Other Senses

Of the five senses—seeing, hearing, touch, smell, and taste—the primary sense used for the enjoyment of mechanical toys is, of course, sight—watching it move. The next is hearing—the noise, sound, or music attached to some toys. The element of touch comes from handling the toy and winding and working it, but touch in itself is rarely the outcome of a toy's action except for vulgar palm-tickling practical jokes or, in earlier days, electric shock machines.

Smell, never used in Western toys, was a feature of ancient Japanese ones, and has been recently revived in scratch-and-sniff greeting cards and novelties. When one of the authors, Athelstan, was commissioner of the Seattle World's Fair and later president of the Franklin Institute in

175. Cover and mechanism of Speaking Book, showing bellows and voice tubes.

Philadelphia, he thought of introducing smell into the museum. The idea was to sit under the night sky of the planetarium dome and have the scent of the piney woods wafted in to enhance the impression of being in the open under the night sky. It did not work. The aroma of the city crowd was overpowering.

Toys that employ the sense of taste were never made. That was left to the child's enjoyment of candy and ice cream and the adult's savoring of gourmet meals and wines.

10
Variety Versus Mass Production

176. Poodle jumping rope directed by bear. Hand-painted tin. Gunthermann, German, circa 1890.

When toy makers were producing a few toys at a time, they could build them with variety. Toward the end of the last century, however, many makers had the idea of making toys cheap enough to put them into the hands of more children. This meant mass production, the antithesis of variety. This problem was solved by many toy makers by mass-producing the basic, expensive parts of power and governing and by varying the uses of these same mass-produced, governed power plants in the different actions that the toys performed.

177. *Le Pêcheur à la ligne* (the angler). Hand-painted tin, rubber-band driven. F. Martin, 1892.

Combination Toys

Gunthermann built clockwork motors with fly fans and plinkety-plink music boxes, all in similar bases, and then placed on those bases different combinations of figures. The same base and music box might have three musicians on a park bench playing different instruments, or a poodle jumping rope (figure 176). By substituting a bellows and squawker for the music box, a clown conducting a singing goose was produced (figure 181). Often different combinations of the same figures were used. This was the solution to introducing diversity into mass production.

The Decamps animals similarly had the same good, expensive clockwork, which was produced in quantity, and different animal forms made of papier-mâché and covered in different skins, which provided diversity (figure 180).

King of the Toy Makers

It might prove instructive in this regard to look at one toy maker in what has been called The Golden Age of Toys, about 1880 to 1910, and see how he coped successfully with this puzzle of supplying many different things to the many.

We could have chosen any of a number of the great toy makers of that era, but we selected the king of them all, Fernand Martin (1849–1919), who worked throughout this period and made many toys, but not too many to be adequately documented. In addition, Martin employed a wide variety of mechanisms with great ingenuity.

Martin's toys are usually divided into three epochs: the first, from 1878 to 1894, with forty-nine toys; the second, from 1895 to 1912, with ninety-one toys; and the final period after 1912, when his company continued but the great inventor was increasingly less active in the manufacturing process.

During the first epoch, more than half of the almost fifty toys Martin made, about thirty, used for their power an elastic band, for their governor a verge escapement, and for the action some kind of a pendulum (figure 177). These are the cheapest and most ingenious kinds of drive, governor, and action for a mechanical toy. In seventeen wheeled toys

during this period, Martin used the identical mechanism of an inertial flywheel spun by hand or with a string to make it travel. In only three did he experiment with more expensive spring wind-up power.

In the second period, almost eighty of Martin's toys were wind-ups, all with essentially the same spring. Even with his wind-up mechanisms, the constraints of mass production caused him to retain the verge escapement as a governor (fig-

178. Mechanism of *Le Gai Violiniste* (the merry violinist), showing spiral spring, verge escapement, and violin-bow pendulum. F. Martin, 1897.

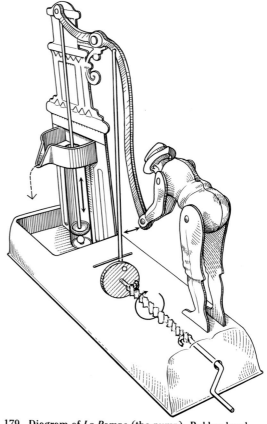

179. Diagram of *La Pompe* (the pump). Rubber-band driven, verge escapement (not shown). Pump handle is pendulum, actually pumps water. F. Martin, 1897.

180. Crocodile walks and moves tail and jaw. Papier-mâché, clockwork. Decamps, French, 1878.

181. Clown conducting singing goose. Hand-painted tin, wind-up with bellows. Gunthermann, German, circa 1890.

ure 178). Martin did produce two marble gravity toys and five with elastic bands (figure 179) or inertial flywheels of the earlier period. However, almost all the toys of the second period were mass-produced wind-up mechanisms.

Although Martin experimented with various mechanisms, he relied mainly on the tried and true devices: elastic bands, flywheels, and simple clockwork. He made only one toy with music—the little pianist. Two hand-operated toys were produced during the first epoch and five in the second. He played with gyroscopes, first in the waltzers, where the woman's skirt was both the inertial power supply and the gyroscope that kept the toy erect, and later with the bicycle.

In Martin there was blended the imagination of the artist and inventor with shrewd business acumen.

182. *Left to right: Le Diable en boîte* (the Devil in the box), 1890; *Le Pêcheur à la ligne*, 1892; *Les Boxeurs* (the boxers), 1891. *Foreground: La Course de taureau* (the bullfight), 1894.

11 Artist in Tinplate

Seraphin Fernand Martin was a country boy who became a leading toy maker in the golden age of toys, the Victorian Age. The little boy had no toys. But he was blessed with an artist's eye, a mechanic's hands, and a mind that appreciated his fellows around him, and even at the age of ten he made his own toys. He grew up to become the king of toy makers, placing beautiful toys in the hands of all his ordinary subjects, not only the privileged few.

He was born in Amiens on April 29, 1849, near the Somme River, seventy-five miles north of Paris. As he played with rubber bands,

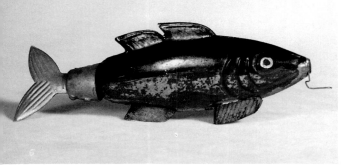

183. *Le Poisson mécanique* (mechanical fish). Hand-painted tin, rubber-band powered. 1878.

184. *Left to right: La Pompe* (the pump), 1897; *Les Courageux Scieurs de long* (the brave long-sawyers), 1886; *Le Sonneur endiablé* (the furious bell ringer), 1885.

bits of wire, and discarded food tins, he fashioned toys which reflected the world he saw around him. The river inspired two of the earliest Martin toys, a man in a boat who could really row and a fish that could really swim.

As early as 1876, Martin sold one of his inventions to manufacturers and his swimming fish appeared in England as Cremer's New Automatic Fish (figure 183). In 1880, he opened his own toy factory in Paris.

Scrap Tin

Almost a century earlier, another French genius in another field had revolution-

ized food preservation. Nicolas Appert, a confectioner, experimented with preserving foodstuffs by heating them in sealed containers. In 1795, the French government offered a 12,000-franc prize to whoever could save foods from one harvest to another. Appert's efforts became known and bottles were used at first. Preserved foods helped Napoleon's army march on its stomach.

Early in the nineteenth century, the can made of steel plated with tin was invented and the Industrial Revolution ushered in the throw-away civilization. Cans replaced bottles in food preservation, and used tin cans abounded in the rubbish dumps of Paris, to be retrieved by rag-and-bone merchants. An industry of *nettoyeurs* (cleansers) boiled the rotten food from the cans in stinking iron cauldrons to salvage clean tin sheets.

People at Work

Martin and other entrepreneurs in the burgeoning industry of mass-produced toys were quick to take advantage of this cheap source of raw materials. Recycled tin was soon crafted into cheap tin toys. The small size of the recycled pieces probably dictated the small size of the Martin toys of the first epoch.

Martin's genius was in the selection of his subjects. He drew these at first from the rural people with whom he had grown up and their occupations. His figures were little caricatures of ordinary people at work—blacksmiths, farriers, bell ringers, plowmen, sawyers, firemen. But Martin's genius also showed in the elegance of his simple mechanisms. Almost all of his toys were powered simply by rubber bands, strings, and inertial flywheels that he had known in his boyhood. The Appendix lists the toys made by Martin during this first epoch, together with power sources and dates.

The twisted rubber band turned a simple version of a verge escapement that had been used for centuries in clocks. The escapement, as in a clock, was the swing of a pendulum, but Martin made the pendulum a part of the action of the toy. Pendulums became the blacksmith's hammer, the bell in the belfry, the rod in the hands of the fisherman, the tail of the fish, the torsos of the pumpers.

With the exception of a few clockwork toys toward the end of this epoch, the keys were simple wire cranks to wind up the rubber bands. During this period when he made forty-nine toys, twenty-seven were actuated by rubber bands, seventeen by flywheels, two by hand, and three were simple wind-up clockworks (figures 182, 184, and 185).

Standardization

Martin was able to manufacture cheaply because he standardized much in his toys even though they were beautifully different in appearance. All the little figures up to 1895 were no more than thirteen centimeters high. All of the torsos and heads, with only two exceptions, were put together from molded halves joined front to back. The legs, arms, and feet were made of a single piece of metal, often flat, sometimes slightly half-molded. All of the toys, except the fish and those on wheels, stood on bases. Only later did Martin learn how to make his little people stand on their own two feet. He used molded and other parts over and over again in different combinations in different toys. The brave long-sawyers are the same figures as the furious bell ringer; the man driving the ostrich is the same as the blacksmith, and has the same mechanism as the delivery man.

During this epoch the figures were all

185. *Left to right: La Forge* (the forge), 1896; *Les Forgerons infatigables* (the tireless blacksmiths), 1883; *Les Joyeux Danseurs* (the happy dancers), 1888; *Le Piocheur* (the pickaxe laborer), 1894.

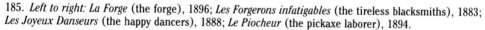

186. *Foreground: Les Valseurs* (the waltzers), 1885. *Left to right: Le Livreur* (the deliveryman), 1888; *Le Pousse-pousse anamite de l'Exposition* (the Annamese rickshaw), 1889; *Le Facteur de chemin de fer* (the railway porter), 1894.

187. *Left to right: La Bicyclette* (the bicycle), 1892; *La Charrette anglaise* (the English trap), 1892; *L'Autruche* (the ostrich cart), 1888; *L'Attelage flamande* (the Flemish dogcart), 1894.

painted, with a few flat surfaces lithographed. Lithography is the term commonly used by toy collectors to describe this coloring process, but in general it is the much more primitive printing art called serigraphy or silk-screening, using paint.

In addition to the rubber band, Martin also used hand-twirled inertial flywheels to supply the energy of movement. All of Martin's wheeled vehicles of this period —the steam carriage, the deliveryman, the ostrich cart, the big drum, the rickshaw, the dogcart, the young cavalier— used hand- or string-twirled inertial flywheels to provide the energy for their movement (figures 186 and 187). However, in two of the early Martins, the flywheel not only did this but also acted as a gyroscope to keep the toy upright as in the waltzers and the bicycle.

Transition

Martin's first toy-making epoch, with all the common features herein described, lasted for a period of sixteen years. In 1895, the second epoch was born. Not only did Martin's subjects now become city people, but as he was probably no longer using scrap tin, the size of his figures almost doubled. The type of clothing changed as well, and although he retained the verge escapement as a governor, the power of his clockwork was a spiral spring.

Fernand Martin, living and working in Paris, had developed a love for the ordinary people of the boulevards. The country boy had become a Parisian, but his eye as an artist, his genius for simple mechanisms, and his gentle caricaturing of ordinary people and their doings continued to shine through.

188. *Left to right: Ma Portière* (my lady doorkeeper), 1895; *La Chasse au rat* (chasing the rat), 1910; *La Casseuse d'assiettes* (the smasher of plates), 1912; *L'Entravée* (the hobble skirt), 1910; *La Danseuse de cakewalk* (the cakewalk dancer), 1903; *La Blanchisseuse* (the washerwoman), 1899.

12 Les Petits Bonshommes Martin

By 1895, Fernand Martin was a citizen of the liveliest, gayest city of the world. He was a boulevardier of Paris, a captain of his industry. With a merry twinkle in his eye, he recorded the doings of his fellow city people. His artist's eye was now augmented by a new invention, an outgrowth of the work of his fellow Frenchmen Niepce (1826) and Daguerre (1839) that was made available to everyone in 1889. Martin took his Kodak camera everywhere.

He obviously took pleasure in his re-creations of the Parisian scene. These, in turn, appealed not only to children but also to grown people in France and, increasingly, in other lands. His toys brought up the sights, sounds, and even the smells of a great city. He was not only a famous inventor but also a chronicler of the people and events that surrounded him.

In his first epoch, Martin's characters had drawn heavily on his early memories of the French countryside. In the second epoch, another span of sixteen years, he drew mainly on city people and current events. He captured the life and spirit of Paris in his little people, the renowned *bonshommes Martins.*

Martin's Little People

Les Petits Bonshommes Martins, the characteristic figures of the second epoch, stood and moved on their own feet.

Petit (small) referred not merely to their size but also to the French connotation of affection for the ordinary people seen on the boulevards of Paris. Indeed, these little walking people literally did spend their time on the boulevards. They were sold on street corners, performing their antics on the pavements, by vendors, who were in turn immortalized in tin, to people who saw their contemporaries in Martin's toys.

Ma Portière, the first of Martin's *petits bonshommes,* was modeled on his concierge, or female doorkeeper, and appeared in 1895. It was almost twice the size of Martin's previous figures and was probably enlarged to house the clockwork in the casing which formed the body. Of the ninety-one toys of this period, seventy-eight were wind-ups. The

189. *Left to right: Le Petit Culbuteur* (the little tumbler), 1908; *Le Pochard* (the drunkard), 1899; *Le Chef d'orchestre* (orchestra leader), 1902; *Les Valseurs* (the waltzers), 1910; *Le Gai Violiniste* (the merry violinist), 1897; *Le Petit Pianiste* (the little pianist), 1902.

190. *Left to right: Le Menuisier* (the carpenter), 1908; *"Chand 'tonneau"* (barrel vendor), 1907; *La Balayeur* (the sweeper), 1899; *L'Artiste capillaire* (the barber), 1902; *Le Faucheur* (the reaper), 1899.

Appendix shows the toys made by Martin during his second epoch from 1895 to 1912.

At Work and Play

Following the success of Ma Portière, *Les Petits Bonshommes Martin* cascaded from his factory at 88 Boulevard de Menilmontant and flooded the market at home and abroad (figure 188). The little people included orchestra leaders, street violinists, washerwomen, drunkards with red noses, delivery boys, policemen, concert pianists, pushcart peddlers, sandwichboard men, soldiers, butchers, barbers, dancers, firemen, lawyers, street vendors, and even a man on a ladder whom some call the Peeping Tom but others, more romantic, think of as the eloper (figures 189, 193, and 195).

Nor did the toy maker neglect chil-

dren's play. The sack race, diabolo, skaters, balloons, schoolboy jockeys, and a recalcitrant student were all chronicled (figure 192), as well as children working while grown men played (figure 191). The peasant coming to the great market of Paris, Les Halles, was not forgotten. Martin celebrated the farmer driving his pigs to market, the vintner rolling his barrels, and the reaper of the wheat for French bread. The nationalistic disdain for the Flemish appeared in a serving girl with a Dutch cap clumsily dropping a stack of plates (figures 188, 190, 194, and 196).

Although there was marked contrast between toys of the first and second epoch in the switch to clockwork and the larger size to contain it, plus the fact that the toys stood on their own feet, Martin adhered to the standardization that had been so successful in his earlier toys. He did make a few taller ones and several with mechanisms other than clockwork (figure 195).

In the larger figures of the second epoch, the join of the stampings for faces and torsos was from ear to ear on the sides, rather than from front to back as in the first epoch's smaller figures.

The Uses of Clothing

By adding cloth costumes, Martin was able to hide simple wire arms and legs. Freestanding figures required heavy lead

191. *Left to right: Le Petit Livreur* (the delivery boy), 1911; *Le Parfait Pêcheur* (the perfect fisherman), 1908; *L' Autopatte* (the apple seller), 1910.

192. *Left to right: L'Intrépide jockey* (the intrepid jockey), 1912; *Le Jeune écuyer* (child riding a chair), 1910; *La Petite Diabolo* (the diabolo player), 1907; *La Course en sac* (the sack race), 1906; *Le Petit Patineur* (the little roller skater), 1912.

193. *Left to right: The Policeman* (English bobby), 1901; *Le Chinois* (the Chinaman), 1900; *L'Éminent Avocat* (the lawyer), 1905; *L'Hercule populaire* (the popular strongman), 1905; *L'Agent de police* (the policeman), 1901.

194. *Left to right: Les Cochons du père François* (Father Francis's pigs), 1910; *Le Petit Cuisinier* (the little cook), 1904; *La Petite Marchande d'oranges* (the little orange vendor), 1901; *Le Charcutier* (the pork butcher), 1902; *"Chaud les marrons"* (hot chestnuts), 1912.

feet for stability. The arms and legs were simple steel wires to which tin hands and lead feet were soldered. In certain cases, dressing in cloth allowed Martin to dispense with arms and even legs, as in the case of Peary at the Pole. Where the hands were attached to an external moving piece, no wire was used; an empty sleeve permitted free movement as in the piano player, the chestnut vendor, and the strongman rolling barrels. The wire limbs and light cloth dress lightened the tops of the toys so that they could maintain their equilibrium on their feet while performing their antics.

The dressing of the toys in cloth was also a masterpiece of simplicity and standardization, suitable for mass production. Cloth was sewn into long tubes, and then appropriate lengths for sleeves and trousers were snipped off with no hems. Often the jacket was a simple piece of material pulled around the neck of a figure with a drawstring.

Where the jacket was formal, as in the tailcoat of the pianist or the orchestra leader, felt was used and cut to hold the shape with no sewing except for the attachment of sleeves. Exceptions are found in the more formal dresses of the ladies in the cakewalk, the waltzing couple, and the diabolo player.

Redressed Martin toys may often be detected by the overkill of hems and seams and other departures from his original simplicity.

Beyond the City

Martin had become a man of the world. He traveled to London and recorded, with his discerning eye and his Kodak, the London bobby and shoeshine boy. He took advantage of and contributed to the Paris Exposition of 1889, which attracted many foreigners, showing the Annamite coolie pulling a lady in a rickshaw, the big drum, and the exposition wheelchair. In 1905, Barnum & Bailey's "Greatest Show on Earth" played in Paris and Martin responded with a toy inspired by the circus's premier attraction, the Mysterious Ball.

Historical events of the day were also noted, mirroring in miniature the front pages of *Le Monde.* The Boer War led to the Man in Khaki; French sympathies were reflected in the Valiant Boer. The establishment of a French colony in Madagascar in 1899 was celebrated by the Colonial Sentry. The tensions in Europe were shown by identical toys in Russian and Italian uniforms. The coronation of King Edward VII, after Queen Victoria's interminable rule, was hailed not only by the British but also by Martin's Little Pianist. Looking much like Paderewski, he played "God Save the King." Edward was popular in France; his mother was not.

Martin's Conquest of the North Pole shows a fur-clad explorer furiously whip-

---

195. *Left to right: Le Treuil* (the winch), marble-activated gravity toy, 1895; *Le Treuil* (the winch), smaller version, 1895; *La Boule mystérieuse* (the mysterious ball), string-wound clockwork, 1906; *Le Joueur de boules* (the bowls player), hand-operated marble roller, 1905; *Le Pompier à l'échelle* (the fireman on the ladder), clockwork inside figure, 1904; *Le Paysan à l'échelle* (the peasant on the ladder), clockwork inside figure, 1904.

196. *Left to right: Le Cab mécanique* (the hansom cab), 1903; *Le Laboureur* (the plowman), 1906; *Les Boeufs* (the oxcart), 1897.

ping his sled dogs around a snow-covered mound surmounted by an American flag (figure 198). Robert E. Peary was the first man to reach the North Pole in 1909, although he survived by eating his sled dogs. The Martin toy is prophetic: his Peary is nearing the pole with only four dogs left.

Flying and Fashion

In 1908 the Wright Brothers were concluding agreements to manufacture their famous airplanes in Europe. By the following year, Martin had manufactured four versions of a toy showing from one to four biplanes flying around a pylon. We have not seen in the literature a reference to the rubber-band version with four biplanes, but there is no question about it being a Martin because the little cast-metal base bears the raised F.M. trademark and is identical to the marble catcher of the large winch.

In an exhibition flight at Anvers-sur-Oise in France, pilot Wilbur Wright carried the first woman airplane passenger. She was an American, Mrs. Hart O. Berg, and against the slipstream, she tied a scarf over her big floppy hat and, being a modest woman, a string around her skirt at the ankles. After the flight, a French couturier, watching her walk away from the plane with the string still tied around her ankles, had the inspiration for the hobble skirt, one of the strangest and most confining garments ever worn by women. It became a fashion fad, making walking almost impossible. Because there were no pockets in the skirt, muffs, used by men to keep their hands warm from ancient times and particularly in the seventeeth and eighteenth centuries, became a necessity for warming the hands as well as for carrying a purse and other accessories.

Martin produced L'Entravée, the lady

in the hobble skirt, with a huge hat and muff, in 1910. Although she was available in both blue and red, the lady in red, which to the English connoted a woman of easy virtue, earned enormous sales in England where she was affectionately known as The Prostitute.

By 1909, when Martin was interviewed for *Playthings*, a trade magazine, his factory was turning out 200,000 of his creations each year, selling for 25 to 30 sous (5 or 6 cents), thus permitting children all over France and in other countries to own a beautiful toy. He said he had invented 130 toys which had brought him 30 prizes at various exhibitions, numerous foreign medals, and France's coveted Cross of the Legion of Honor. The country boy had become an esteemed citizen of France, a character loved and looked up to by children of France and envied but respected by competitors at home and abroad.

Flersheim Takes Over

Fernand Martin had been grooming his only son, Maurice, to take over his business, and began to rely on him for assistance in creating his little people. But in 1907, at the age of thirty-five, Maurice fell seriously ill, probably from tuberculosis. Martin left Paris with his family for the south of France in 1908. In 1912, he sold his factory to Georges Flersheim, the twenty-two-year-old son of an important banking family. Martin's creations continued in production with the advice of the creator for a number of years. The toys manufactured during this time are listed in the Appendix.

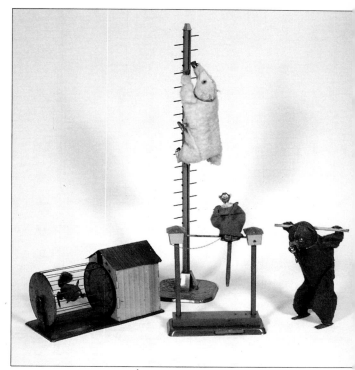

197. *Left to right: Le Petit Écureuil vivant* (the little live squirrel), 1908; *L'Ours blanc* (white bear climbing a pole), 1909; *La Danse des Singes* (the dancing monkey), 1908; *L'Ours Martin* (the Martin bear), brown or white, 1903.

198. *Left to right: La Conquête de pôle Nord* (the conquest of the North Pole), clockwork, 1909; *L'Aéroplane* (two biplanes), compression spring, 1909; *Les Aéroplanes* (four biplanes), rubber band, 1909.

However, Flersheim caused controversy and litigation by claiming a number of Martin's patents for his own. Ironically, Flersheim was killed when a cannon of his own invention exploded while he was serving as lieutenant of artillery in Belgium in 1915.[19] He was literally "hoist with his own petar."

Fernard Martin's toy enterprise was acquired in 1919 by his old friend Francis Victor Bonnet, and continued under the name of Victor Bonnet et Cie until 1965.

Martin died September 1, 1919, just two weeks after the death of his son Maurice.[20] Except for the toys from Fernand Martin's inventory that later bore the V.B. et Cie imprint, his successors' contributions bear witness to the fact that Bonnet purchased Fernand Martin's company but not his genius.

13
Followers and Imitators

199. *Rear left: #248 V.B. & Cie Les Auto-Transports* and *#250 Tracteur avec remorque* (road tractor with covered cab with cloth-covered trailer). *Rear right: #246 Le Déverseur* (the dump truck). *Foreground: #254 Le Train tortillard* (road tractor towing four trailers).

After Victor Bonnet took over Fernand Martin's toy company in 1919, he concentrated at first on selling the inventory of Martin toys, and continued to manufacture at least ten of them. Most of these were sold in the Martin boxes without even the imprint of V.B. & Cie. Succrs. Later on, he left off the Succrs.

These toys are shown in a 1928 catalogue, *Les Jouets Mécaniques de Fernand Martin,* published by Victor Bonnet & Cie. Succrs., Paris. The numbers are the same as the Martin numbers. The Appendix lists these toys.

Some of these reissues show slight modifications. For instance, the bear is white instead of Martin's brown; the fireman on the ladder wears a different helmet that does not cover the back of his neck; the delivery boy has differently labeled packages, and his cart's wheels are solid rather than spoked.

Most of the V.B.'s carried a small rectangular brass or round lithographed plate with V.B. & Cie. The bear, however, was imprinted on its foot.

Trucks and Pistols

The character of the toys changed when Victor Bonnet started making his own. Remembering that this was shortly after World War I, it is not surprising that Bonnet turned to warlike cap pistols, trucks,

200. *Ma Portière (left)* and German version.

201. *Left to right:* #255 *La Charrette paysanne* (horse-drawn peasant cart), 1927; #263 *La Patinette,* boy on scooter, 1929; #253, *Le Clown orchestre,* clown with bells seated on piano, operated by depressing piano keys, 1927; #252, *L'Homme-toupie,* clown standing on head twirls on hat, 1924; #265, *La Voiture nounou,* nurse pushing pram with baby, 1929; #259, *L'Entraineur "Skiff,"* boy riding three-wheeled cart, 1928.

202. Bonnet's wood pigeons, two versions.

203. Martin *(left)* and Gunthermann waltzing couples.

trailers, and automobiles, although it is said that Fernand Martin never accepted self-propelled vehicles and only traveled by horse-drawn carriage or by train (figure 199).

In the Series Les Auto-Transports, Bonnet carried on Martin's method of reusing and recombining component parts for subsequent toys, and even made it possible for children to assemble different toys themselves. His trucks are all basically the same, differing only in being open or closed or carrying a fixed or tilting bed. By moving the rear wheels forward and eliminating the bed altogether, he created a tractor which was sold alone or in combination with various trailers.

At least one of the old Martins was later made from original molds and given a new number. The girl with plates

204. Martin tumbler *(left)* and German version.

205. Martin's delivery man *(left)* and the German Lehmann Express.

206. Martin's hansom cab *(left)* and German version by Ullmann & Engelmann.

was named Madelon. A cloth blouse and apron covered the original painted metal dress, and the plates were decorated with stars. There was also a version with just one fixed plate piled with fruit. The reissued Madelon was numbered 260 and carried no imprint, whereas Martin's original was numbered 233 with FM embossed on the cap.

Among the toys Victor Bonnet made are a few with some of the charm of Martin: for example, the clown standing on its head, the horse-drawn peasant cart, the three-wheeled skiff, the nurse pushing the pram, and a rather anachronistic one often taken for much older than it really is, a clown seated on a piano who rings bells when keys are depressed. Even these do not have the delicacy of the Martins. V.B. toys tended to be larger and heavier and more lacking in proportion (figure 201).

These toys, nineteen designed by Bon-

net and the reissue mentioned above, are listed in the Appendix.

Bonnet's firm continued and, according to Pressland,[21] produced tin road vehicles with the trademark VEBE in the 1940s and 1950s. There was also a series of perhaps seven wood pigeons called Le Ramier with modern clockwork which appeared under the V.B. et Cie label in 1922 and continued from 1938 until 1945 under the VEBE label (figure 202). Some soldered joints in the earlier versions were replaced with tin tabs and were lithographed rather than hand-painted in a uniform color with a few contrasting details. The plain cardboard box was simply stamped "Pigeon, Ramier, No.——."

Competition and Copying

In the years preceding the start of World War I, French and German manufacturers of mechanical toys continued and intensified the fierce competition for markets at home and abroad. What we now call industrial espionage was rampant, with toy makers quickly copying each others' newest creations, buying ideas from young inventors for very small amounts, and even indulging in a bit of blatant patent infringement.

Martin's successful toys were often copied, principally by other French and German manufacturers. This is not to say that Martin, entrepreneur that he was, did not himself indulge in a little piracy. When Martin presented his collection to the Conservatoire des Arts et Métiers in 1908, all of Paris flocked to see the works of the master and a scandal ensued.

A toy shop owner named Foucault

207. Organ grinder. Lithographed metal with composition head, music. S.I.J.I.M., French, 1911.

said he had given many ideas to Martin before the turn of the century. Boucher claimed credit for a billiard player said to have been produced by Martin. Paulet was unhappy with the paltry sum he received for his acrobat. Jeannet claimed Martin stole his dancing monkey and his monkey on a swing. Gasselin insisted that the perfect fisherman, the mysterious ball, and the bowls player were his own. Bousquet said he invented the little pianist and that Martin merely changed the tune.[22]

Regardless of who copied from whom, there are, as a result, pitfalls for the Martin collector.

Lookalikes

Most notable among the lookalikes are Martin's Ma Portière and a German version (figure 200). Similar walking figures include an old woman in wire-rimmed spectacles carrying a basket on her back, Busy Lizzie with a carpet sweeper or broom, a woman going to market with an umbrella and basket, and a lady gardener. Martin's woman chasing a mouse with a broom also appears in a German version.

Martin's waltzing couple and Gunthermann's waltzers (figure 203) are quite similar, as are Martin's 1889 hansom cab and the slightly larger Ullmann & Engelmann version of about 1900 (figure 206). The Martin tumbler and its German counterpart are alike in scale and action and, as in the case of the waltzers, the Martins are cloth-dressed whereas the German versions are hand-painted (figure 204).

The most extraordinary lookalikes are Martin's delivery man and the Lehmann Express, and Martin's ostrich cart and Lehmann's various ostrich-drawn carts (figures 205 and 208). As far as we can tell, Lehmann's Express and ostrich cart appeared in about the same year as Martin's, 1888. Martin's rickshaw was first

208. Martin's ostrich cart *(left)* and Lehmann's ostrich cart.

produced in 1889, five years before Lehmann's Mikado Family.

Hillier shows us a peacock, distinguishable from the common German versions by the fact that it stands on its own two feet without side supports, and attributes it to Martin. She also asserts that the German billiard player hitting balls fed from under the table into holes marked with various scores is more commonly found than the Martin version.[23] We have never seen evidence that Martin produced either of these toys. However, we have not given up the hope that someday, somewhere, we will find them.

The confusion is further compounded by the different printing on the boxes for sale in foreign countries. Martin's swimming fish, one of his earliest toys, was sold in England as Cremer's New Automatic Fish, and was later copied in a larger and very nice toy by the firm L. J. M. of Paris, which received a gold medal for it at the Concours L'Epine about the turn of the century. A 1915 article in a French trade publication compared the French and German toy industries at that time.[24] Although the popular belief that an immense number of French toys were being marked "made in Germany" is apparently unfounded, we must conclude that at least some were so marked to facilitate sale to foreign markets.

A great 1911 toy of an organ grinder playing a street organ (figure 207) is so Martinlike in its charm and caricature that it is often thought to be a Martin, although the music box is marked S.I.J.I.M.—for the Société Industrielle de Jouets et Inventions Mécaniques, which

209. Old man in brown coat. Resembles Martin's *Le Vieux Marcheur.* Probably German, circa 1902.

210. Chinaman with gong. Hand-painted tin. European; Indian with bow. Hand-painted tin. European, circa 1910.

211. Buffalo Bill. Hand-painted, hand-operated, lever-actuated. Probably French, circa 1900.

212. Redcoat and Boer, wind-up. Reversing mechanism under Redcoat causes him to alternately advance and retreat. Probably German, circa 1900.

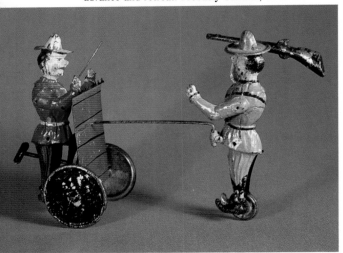

was founded in Paris in about 1900.

There are other toys that have the charm and ingenuity and may even have the characteristic lead feet of the Martins. The painted tin Indian with his bow and arrow and the pink-coated Chinaman striking a gong (figure 210) wobble along like the Bonshommes Martins. A walking clockwork figure of a man in a brown coat with gray top hat (figure 209) has lead feet and wire legs, although the feet are solid to the knee. The figure of Buffalo Bill (figure 211) resembles that of the bowls player and stands on a crude Martinlike tin base similar to that of the perfect fisherman.

A reversible toy with a Boer carrying a rifle and a Redcoat behind a breastwork alternately chasing each other (figure 212) is so beautiful that for a long time we thought it was Martin's Valiant Boer, but now we know it is not.

The gyroscopic top in the shape of a dancing couple made by Martin in 1885 is almost identical to the one made by or at least sold by Ives in this country.

A recent London auction catalogue offered "A Fernand Martin Swimming Doll, American, circa 1890," which turned out to be French and, in fact, manufactured by a Monsieur Martin. This Parisian toy maker was Elie Martin, who produced the swimming doll called Ondine in 1876 (figure 118).

With this confusion, the collector should not be impatient with dealers or auction houses which attribute to Martin beautiful toys that are not of his manufacture. It is not at all easy to be sure.

213. Four-man scull with coxswain. Tin litho wind-up. George Levy, Nürnberg, German, circa 1920.

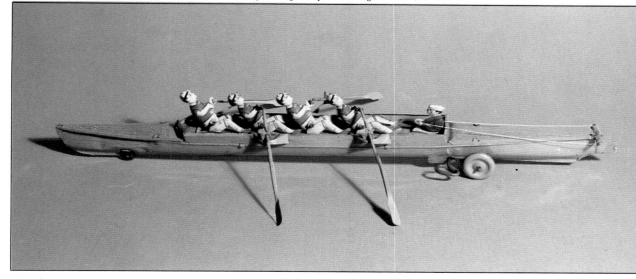

Afterword

Everyone asks why we collect toys. The answer is simple: We enjoy them. We appreciate their art, their humor, their ingenuity, their music, and their place in history. Governments and organizations preserve the heritage of the great, but any collectors, no matter what they collect, can preserve the heritage of ordinary people.

Barnaby Conrad, in an article on lost masterpieces of art and literature, quotes the Spanish proverb "Let that which is lost be for God," but goes on to admit to being "a trifle envious and a little

214. Woman at sewing machine. Hand-painted tin, clockwork. Gunthermann, German, circa 1900.

resentful of the Great Collector in the sky with his full gallery and library."[25]

He must also have a fine collection of toys up there, considering how many are rare because of loss or destruction.

Many toy collectors don't care whether their toys work or not. We do. Just as its historical relationship is part of a toy's appeal, so is our knowledge of its innards. Fixing and operating them gives the added satisfaction of working with the hands.

As we have said before, your hand in the world of mechanical toys is like the sun in the real world. Your hand's energy is stored in toys by springs, flywheels, and weights just as the sun's is stored on our planet. And there's another consid-

215. Horse race. Hand-painted tin, wind-up. German, circa 1900.

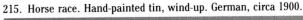

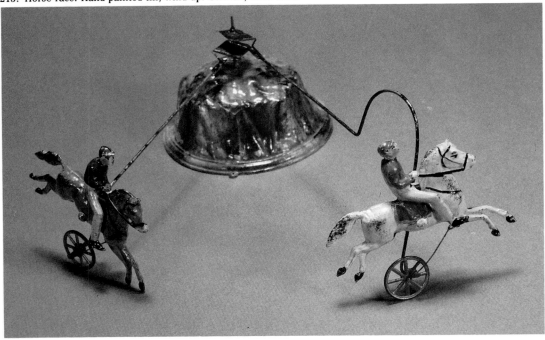

eration that explains our enjoyment of handwork. When humans first stood upright, they liberated their prehensile hands. They could then grasp and make tools. From this sprang the technology to free them from hard hand labor. In their free hands they could at last grasp toys —tools that made priceless smiles and laughter.

Although the variety of toys is almost limitless, colorful hand-held, hand-operated, hand-wound toys are still our favorites. If, in addition to these tactile and visual virtues, a toy portrays people or animals and adds the further wonder of tinkling music or animal noises, this is the epitome.

Those who have lost touch with fan-

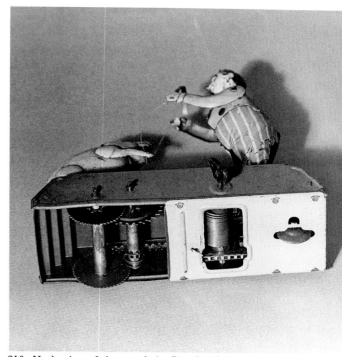

216. Mechanism of clown and pig. Barrel spring and ratchet reversing gear.

217. Clown and pig. Tin litho, wind-up. German, circa 1910.

tasy often ask what a toy is worth. It is true that many toys, particularly old and rare ones, command a high price. But they are worth only as much as you cherish them, admire them, play with them, and derive pleasure from them. An investment in toys, great or small, pays interest daily in the golden coin of joy.

218. Bisque head, shoulder doll on wheeled platform with flower basket, clockwork. European, circa 1910.

219. Clown on hands. Hand-painted tin, clockwork. German, circa 1890.

Acknowledgments

We want to thank *Smithsonian* magazine, particularly its editors Ed Thompson and Don Moser; *Technology Review* and its editor John Mattill; the *Encyclopaedia Britannica* and its *Yearbook* editors David Calhoun and Kathy Nakamura; and *Antique Toy World* and its editor Dale Kelley. These fine publishers encouraged us to write about toys and offered their fullest cooperation in the preparation of this book.

The friends, collectors, and dealers, often all three in the same person, who have shared their knowledge and helped us collect, enjoy, and understand toys are too numerous to be listed. We just

ACKNOWLEDGMENTS

mention a few for special thanks, includ-ing Tony Annese, Barney Barenholtz, Bill and Lillian Gottschalk, Earnie and Ida Long, Inez McClintock, Ginnie Moore, Paul and Stephie Sadagursky, Bob and Marianne Schneider, Curt and Linda Smith, Frank and Fran Whitson, Blair Whitton, and all the members of the Antique Toy Collectors of America.

At Crown Publishers we would like to thank our editor Ann Cahn, as well as June Bennett, Mark McCauslin, and Milt Wackerow.

Finally, this book could not have been done without the painstaking photography of our friend and neighbor Nelson McClary, who has spent many, many days over a span of more than ten years photographing our toys.

Appendix

Toys of Fernand Martin, First Epoch (1878–1894)

Power source:
RB = rubber band; F = flywheel; H = hand; CW = clockwork;
G = gravity (marbles); U = unknown; FM# = Martin's number

DATE	POWER	TOY
1878	RB	*Le Poisson mécanique,* mechanical fish.
1880	RB	*Le Bateau godilleur,* sculling boat.
1881	RB	*La Balancoire,* monkey on swing.
1881	RB	*Le Bouquet surprise,* bouquet springs from box.
1881	RB	*La Grenouille amphibie,* swimming frog.
1882	RB	*Le Pantin mécanique,* mechanical jumping jack.
1883	RB	*Les Forgerons infatigables,* tireless blacksmiths.
1883	RB	*Le Moulin mécanique à tic-tac,* mechanical windmill.
1883	F	*La Locomotive routière,* floor locomotive.
1884	RB	*Le Cheval à bascule,* rocking horse.
1884	F	*Le Vélocipède,* tricycle.
1884	H	*Le Jeu de force,* devil pops from pole.
1885	RB	*Le Trapèze,* acrobat on swing.
1885	RB	*Le Sonneur endiablé,* furious bell ringer.
1885	F	*Les Valseurs,* waltzing couple top, two versions.
1885	H	*Le Jeu de massacre,* cardboard target game.
1886	RB	*La Danseuse de corde,* tightrope dancer.
1886	RB	*Les Courageux Scieurs de long,* brave long-sawyers.
1887	RB	*Les Fameux Duellistes,* famous duellists.
1887	RB	*Les Pompiers,* two firemen working pump.
1887	RB	*Les Jeu de bascule,* two figures on seesaw.
1888	F	*Le Livreur,* deliveryman pulling cart.
1888	RB	*Les Joyeux Danseurs,* happy dancers on rods.
1888	F	*L'Autruche,* ostrich cart.
1889	F	*Le Cab,* hansom cab (clockwork after 1903).
1889	CW	*L'Écrevisse,* crayfish.
1889	F	*Le Fauteuil roulant de l'Exposition universelle,* porter pushing lady in wheeled chair.
1889	F	*Le Pousse-pousse anamite de l'Exposition universelle,* coolie pulling lady in rickshaw.
1889	F	*La Grosse caisse de l'Exposition universelle,* drummer and bass drum on stand.
1889	RB	*La Grosse caisse automatique de l'Exposition universelle,* drummer pushing bass drum on wheels.
1890	F	*La Sauteuse de corde,* girl skipping rope.
1890	RB	*Le Lapin vivant,* lively rabbit, wire crank in nose.
1890	F	*Le Lapin vivant,* lively rabbit, flywheel twirler on side.
1890	RB	*Le Diable en boîte,* devil in box.
1890	F	*Don Quichotte,* Don Quixote on horse.

DATE	POWER	TOY
1891	RB	*Les Boxeurs,* boxers on platform.
1892	CW	*La Perruche,* parakeet (two color variants).
1892	RB	*Le Pêcheur à la ligne,* fisherman on boat.
1892	RB	*Le Shérif,* sheik riding camel.
1892	F	*Le Charrette anglaise,* boy pulling two children in English fore-and-aft trap.
1892	CW	*Le Traineau russe,* horse-drawn Russian sleigh.
1892	F	*La Bicyclette,* bicycle.
1892	F	*Le Courrier parisien,* Parisian messenger rides horse pulling cart.
1893	RB	*La Chaloupe à vapeur,* steam launch.
1893	RB	*Le Perroquet,* parrot on swinging perch.
1894	F	*L'Attelage flamande,* Flemish dogcart.
1894	RB	*Le Piocheur,* pickaxe man.
1894	RB	*La Course de taureau,* bullfight (later version clockwork).
1894	F	*Le Facteur de chemin de fer,* railway porter.

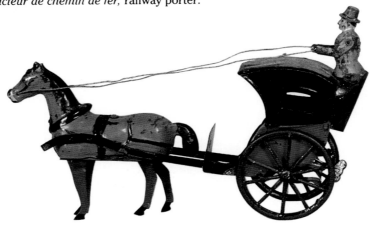

Toys of Fernand Martin, Second Epoch (1895–1912)

DATE	POWER	FM#	TOY
1895	CW/RB	147	*Ma Portière,* my lady doorkeeper (rubber-band version rare).
1895	CW/RB	148	*La Sauteur intrépide,* intrepid jumper leaps over bar.
1895	G	149	*Le Treuil,* winch, marble toy, separate catch basin, 65 cm.
1895	G		*Le Treuil,* winch, marble toy, integral catch basin, 48.5 cm.
1896	H		*L'Araignée et la mouche,* spider chasing fly on string.
1896	CW		*La Mouche,* the fly.
1896	RB		*La Forge,* blacksmiths at forge marked "Marechal Ferrant."
1896	U		*L'Assiette au beurre,* jumping jack throwing butter plate (no known examples).
1896	H		*Le Monocycle aérien,* unicycle on string.
1896	RB		*Le Manège de cochons,* carousel with pigs.
1897	CW		*La Famille vélo,* the cycling family.
1897	CW	160	*Le Gai Violiniste,* merry violinist.
1897	F		*Les Boeufs,* oxcart.
1897	RB		*La Pompe,* man working water pump.
1897	CW		*Le Lapin tambour (Le Lapin agile),* rabbit with drum.
1898	CW	167	*Le Petit décrotteur,* shoeshine boy.

DATE	POWER	FM#	TOY
1898	CW		*Le Motocycle*, man on tricycle pulls lady in carriage.
1899	CW	169	*L'Oie*, walking goose.
1899	CW		*Le Faucheur*, reaper with scythe.
1899	CW	171	*La Blanchisseuse*, washerwoman.
1899	CW	172	*Le Balayeur (Le Portier)*, sweeper, flat-brimmed hat.
1899	CW	172bis	*Le Pochard*, drunkard.
1900	CW	173	*L'Homme de corvée*, soldier in red fatigue cap with broom.
1900	CW		*Le Chinois*, Chinaman with sword and spear.
1900	CW		*Le Vaillant Boer*, valiant Boer with rifle.
1900	CW		*Le Gentleman khaki*, British soldier of Boer War in khaki.
1901	CW		*The Sentinel*, British Royal Palace Guard in shako.
1901	CW	178	*L'Agent de police*, Parisian traffic policeman with baton.
1901	CW	179	*Bamboula*, black man dances and waves arms.
1901	CW		*Présentez armes*, English redcoat with rifle.
1901	CW		*The Policeman*, English bobby directs traffic.
1901	CW		*Le Garçon de café*, black waiter with tray.
1901	CW		*Le Télégraphiste*, postman.
1901	CW		*Le Charbonnier*, coal man with sack on left shoulder (same man as Le Fort de la halle, below).
1901?	CW		*La Course de taureau*, bullfight (same as 1894, above, bullfight but CW).
1901	CW	183	*La Sentinelle française*, French sentry.
1901	CW	184	*La Petite Marchande d'oranges*, orange vendor.
1902	CW	185	*Le Vieux Marcheur*, old man with cane and cigar.
1901	CW	186	*L'Homme-sandwich*, man with sandwich boards.
1902	CW	187	*Le Charcutier*, pork butcher, two cleavers, three-legged chopping block.
1902	CW		*Le Fort de la halle*, strongman of the market (same as Le Charbonnier, above, but with sack on his back).
1902	CW		*La Sentinelle russe*, Russian soldier.
1902	CW		*La Sentinelle coloniale (La Sentinelle orientale)*, French colonial soldier in turban.
1902	CW		*La Sentinelle italienne*, Italian soldier.
1902	CW	189	*Le Petit Pianiste*, little pianist, (4 versions: male or female figure, plays "J'ai du bon tabac" or "God Save the King").
1902	CW	190	*Le Clown antipodiste*, clown walking on hands.
1902	CW		*Le Chef d'orchestre*, orchestra leader.
1903	CW	191	*Le Gendarme*, French policeman with Napoleon style hat.
1903	CW	192	*Le Cab mécanique*, same as 1889 cab but CW.
1903	CW	193	*L'Ours Martin*, Martin bear, brown or white.
1904	CW	194	*La Voiture à bitume*, horse-drawn asphalt cart.
*1903	CW	195	*La Danseuse de cakewalk*, cakewalk dancer.
1902	CW	196	*L'Artiste capillaire*, barber.
1904	CW	197	*Le Paysan à l'échelle*, peasant on ladder.
1904	CW	197bis	*Le Pompier à l'échelle*, fireman on ladder.
1904	CW	198	*Le Petit Cuisinier*, chef cutting carrot.
1905	H	199	*Le Joueur de boules*, bowler.
1905	CW	200	*L'Hercule populaire*, weightlifter.
1905	CW	201	*Le Gymnaste*, gymnast on parallel bars.
1905	CW	202	*L'Éminent Avocat*, eminent lawyer in black or judge in red robes.
1906	CW	203	*Le Laboureur*, farmer with horse-drawn plow.
1906	CW	204	*La Boule mystérieuse*, mysterious ball (string-wound).

DATE	POWER	FM#	TOY
1906	CW	205	*La Course en sac,* sack race.
1907	H	206	*La Pêche à la grenouille sauteuse,* game of fishing for four frogs with hook and line.
1907	CW	207	*"Chand 'tonneau,"* barrel vendor.
1907	CW	208	*Le Joueur de diabolo,* the diabolo player (two versions, boy or girl).
1908	CW	209	*Le Parfait Pêcheur,* perfect fisherman.
1908	CW	210	*Le Boucher,* butcher with pig's head on his hat.
1908	CW	211	*Le Petit Écureuil vivant,* squirrel in cage.
1908	CW	212	*Le Menuisier,* carpenter.
1908	CW	213	*Le Petit Culbuteur,* little tumbler.
1908	CW	214	*La Danse des singes,* dancing monkey, string wound.
1909	H	215	*L'Aéroplane,* one or two biplanes on tower, compression spring.
1909?	RB		*Les Aéroplanes,* four biplanes on pylon.
1909	CW	216	*L'Ours blanc,* white bear climbing pole.
1909	CW	217	*La Conquête du pôle,* conquest of the Pole.
1910	CW	218	*L'Autopatte,* apple cart pushed by feet.
1910	CW	219	*Les Valseurs,* waltzing couple.
1910	CW	220	*L'Entravée,* lady in hobble skirt (red or blue).
1910	CW	221	*La Chasse au rat,* woman chasing rat with broom.
1910	CW	222	*Le Jeune écuyer,* schoolboy riding a chair.
1911	CW	223	*La Jupe-culotte,* lady in breeches.
1911	CW	224	*Le Petit Livreur,* delivery boy pushing cart, with box labeled *"colis parisien très très pressé."*
1912	CW	225	*L'Intrépide Jockey,* intrepid jockey.
1912	CW	225bis	*Vol de la Joconde,* theft of the Mona Lisa (same as above but jockey carries painting).
1910	CW	226	*Les Cochons du père François,* Father Francis and his pigs.

Toys Appearing During the Flersheim Period (1912–1916)

Martin Toys that Reached the Market After Flersheim's Takeover

DATE	POWER	FM#	TOY
1912	CW	227	*"Chaud les Marrons,"* chestnut vendor.
1912	CW	228	*Le Motocycliste enragé,* cyclist in hoop.
1912	CW	229	*Le Petit Patineur,* roller skater.
1912	CW	231	*La Motocyclette,* man on three-wheeled motorcycle, spoked lead wheels.
1912	CW	233	*La Casseuse d'assiettes,* smasher of plates (red or blue skirt).

Other Toys Introduced During the Flersheim Period

DATE	POWER	FM#	TOY
1912		230	*La Pédalette* (no information available).
1912	CW	232	*La Soldat bulgare,* the Bulgarian soldier.
1912	CW		*Le Cab,* hansom cab, same as FM#192, blue version.
1912			*Le Monocycle,* the unicycle.
1913	H		*La Ferme,* the farm, box of lead figures.
1913	CW		*La Nurse,* nursemaid carrying baby.
1914	CW		*La Sentinelle américaine,* the American soldier.
1914	CW	240	*La Guerre aérienne,* aerial dogfight, same biplane as #215 with German monoplane attached.

DATE	POWER	FM#	TOY
1916	H		*La Mitraillette,* lead machine gun.
1916	RB	246	*"Je sonne la paix"* ("I ring peace"), same as 1885 bell ringer, base marked with new name.

Martin Toys Shown in 1928 Catalogue of Victor Bonnet & Cie.

FM#	TOY
160	*Le Gai Violiniste,* violinist.
172bis	*Le Pochard,* drunkard.
184	*La Petite Marchande d'oranges,* street vendor with oranges.
185	*La Petite Marchande,* street vendor with cart.
193	*L'Ours Martin,* bear.
197bis	*Le Pompier à l'échelle,* fireman on ladder.
213	*Le Petit Culbuteur,* tumbler.
218	*L'Autopatte,* cart propelled by feet of boy.
224	*Le Petit Livreur,* delivery boy, box labeled *"je fais le tour du monde."*
231	*La Motocyclette,* motorcycle, solid wheels.

Toys Made by Victor Bonnet

FM#	TOY
246	*Le Déverseur* (series Les Auto-Transports), dump truck.
247	*Le Pan! Pan!,* cap pistol.
248	*Le Tracteur* (series Les Auto-Transports), road tractor with covered cab, sold with various trailers.
249	*Le Camion roulant* (series Les Auto-Transports), two-axled truck with open cab and low-sided bed.
250	*La Remorque* (series Les Auto-Transports), cloth-covered trailer marked Service Rapide, sold with tractor #248.
251	*Le Ramier,* wood pigeon.
252	*L'Homme-toupie,* clown standing on head twirls on hat.
253	*Le Clown orchestre,* clown with bells seated on piano, operated by depressing piano keys.
254	*Le Train tortillard* (series Les Auto-Transports), twisting highway train: four carts towed by tractor similar to #248 but with open cab; cart marked Nice carries bricks; Bordeaux a wine keg; other carts marked Strasburg and Lens.
255	*La Charette paysanne,* horse-drawn peasant cart.
256	*Le Flac!,* cap pistol.
257	*La Bombarde,* cap pistol.
258	*Le Pétard,* cap pistol.
259	*L'Entraineur "Skiff,"* boy riding three-wheeled cart.
260	*Madelon casseuse d'assiettes,* girl with plates (reissue of FM#233).
261	*Le Camion* (series Les Auto-Transports), same truck as #249 but with cab roof and cloth-covered bed marked "Gros Camionnage."
262	*Le Tape-fort,* cap pistol.
263	*La Patinette,* boy on scooter.
264	*Le Sans balle* (no information available).
265	*La Voiture nounou,* baby nurse pushing pram.

Notes

1. Jurgen and Marianne Cieslik, *Lehmann Toys, The History of E. P. Lehmann—1881–1981* (London: New Cavendish Books, 1982), pp. 96–97.

2. Mary Hillier, *Automata and Mechanical Toys* (London: Jupiter Books, 1976), pp. 61, 139.

3. Alfred Chapius and Edmond Droz, *Automata* (Neuchatel: Editions du Griffon, 1958), pp. 289 ff.

4. Ibid.

5. Hillier, op. cit., p. 55.

6. Christian Bailly, *Automata, The Golden Age, 1848–1914* (London: Sotheby's Publications, Philip Wilson, and New York: Harper and Row, 1987), pp. 113–54.

7. Ibid., pp. 272–333.

8. Charles Bartholomew, *Mechanical Toys* (Secaucus, N.J.: Chartwell Books, 1979), p. 32.

9. Brian Moran, *Battery Toys* (Exton, Pa.: Schiffer Publishing, Ltd., 1984), p. 41.

10. Blair Whitton, *American Clockwork Toys, 1862–1900* (Exton, Pa.: Schiffer Publishing, Ltd., 1981), pp. 101–23.

11. Hillier, op. cit., pp. 36–43; diagram of Karakuri tumbler, p. 40.

12. Leslie Daiken, *Children's Toys Throughout the Ages* (London: Spring Books, 1963), p. 37.

13. Ibid., p. 48.

14. Al Davidson, *Penny Lane, A History of Antique Mechanical Toy Banks* (Mokelumne Hill, Calif.: Long's Americana, 1987); and Bill Norman, *The Bank Book, An Encyclopedia of Mechanical Bank Collecting* (San Diego: Accent Studios, 1984).

15. Hillier (op. cit., pp. 145–46) tells us that Ondine was invented by Bertran and produced by E. Martin; Whitton (op. cit., pp. 149–51) says it was invented by Martin and produced by Bertran.

16. Cieslik, op. cit., pp. 194, 206.

17. Daiken, op. cit., p. 27.

18. Chapius and Droz, op. cit., pp. 320–26.

19. Frederic Marchand, *The History of Martin Mechanical Toys* (Paris: Editions l'Automobiliste, 1987), pp. 20–24.

20. Ibid.

21. David Pressland, *The Art of the Tin Toy* (New York: Crown Publishers, 1976), p. 220.

22. Hillier, op. cit., pp. 162–75.

23. Ibid.

24. Georges d'Avenal, "Jouets Français contre Jouets Allemands," *Revue des Deux Mondes*, May 15, 1915, p. 343.

25. Barnaby Conrad, "A Woeful Gallery of the World's Lost Masterpieces," *Smithsonian*, November 1987, p. 258.

Bibliography

Baecker, Carlernst, and Deiter Haas. *Die Anderen Nürnberger, Technisches Spielzeug aus der "Guten Alten Zeit."* Frankfurt: Hobby Haas, Vol. I, 1973; II, 1973; III, 1974; IV, 1975; V, 1976; VI, with Christian Väterlein, 1981.

————, and Christian Väterlein. *Vergessenes Blechspielzeug, Germany's Forgotten Toymakers.* Frankfurt: Frankfurter Fachbuchhandlung Michael Kohl, 1982.

Bailly, Christian. *Automata, The Golden Age, 1848–1914.* London: Sotheby's Publications, Philip Wilson Publishers, Ltd.; and New York: Harper and Row, 1987.

Barenholtz, Bernard, and Inez McClintock. *American Antique Toys, 1830–1900.* New York: Harry N. Abrams, 1980.

Barenholtz, Edith F., ed. *The George Brown Toy Sketchbook.* Princeton, N.J.: The Pyne Press, 1971.

Bartholomew, Charles. *Mechanical Toys.* Secaucus, N.J.: Chartwell Books, 1979.

Chapius, Alfred, and Edmond Droz. *Automata.* Neuchatel: Editions du Griffon, 1958.

Cieslik, Jurgen and Marianne. *Lehmann Toys, The History of E. P. Lehmann—1881–1981.* London: New Cavendish Books, 1982.

Conrad, Barnaby. "A Woeful Gallery of the World's Lost Masterpieces." *Smithsonian* magazine, November 1987.

Daiken, Leslie. *Children's Toys Throughout the Ages.* London: Spring Books, 1963.

d'Avenal, Georges. "Jouets Français contre Jouets Allemands." *Revue des Deux Mondes,* May 15, 1915.

Davidson, Al. *Penny Lane, A History of Antique Mechanical Toy Banks.* Mokelumne Hill, Calif.: Long's Americana, 1987.

deCamp, L. Sprague. *The Ancient Engineers.* Cambridge, Mass.: The M.I.T. Press, 1970.

Gottschalk, Lillian. *American Toy Cars & Trucks.* New York: Abbeville Press, 1985.

Hertz, Louis H. *The Handbook of Old American Toys.* Wethersfield, Conn.: Mark Haber & Co., 1947.

————. *The Toy Collector.* New York: Hawthorne Books, 1976.

Hillier, Mary. *Automata & Mechanical Toys.* London: Jupiter Books, 1976.

Jeanmaire, Claude. *Gebrüder Bing, Spielzeug zur Vorkreigszeit 1912–1915.* Nürnberg: Gebrüder Bing, 1977.

King, Constance Eileen. *The Encyclopedia of Toys.* New York: Crown Publishers, 1978.

Levy, Allen, ed. *The Great Toys of Georges Carette.* London: New Cavendish Books, 1975.

Long, Earnest and Ida. *Dictionary of Toys Sold in America.* Mokelumne Hill, Calif.: Long's Americana, Vol. I, 1971; Vol. II, 1978.

Marchand, Frederic. *The History of Martin Mechanical Toys.* Paris: Editions l'Automobiliste, 1987.

McClintock, Inez and Marshall. *Toys in America.* Washington, D.C.: Public Affairs Press, 1961.

Milet, Jacques, and Robert Forbes. *Toy Boats, 1870–1955, A Pictorial History.* New York: Charles Scribner's Sons, 1979.

Moran, Brian. *Battery Toys.* Exton, Pa.: Schiffer Publishing, Ltd., 1984.

Norman, Bill. *The Bank Book, An Encyclopedia of Mechanical Bank Collecting.* San Diego, Calif.: Accent Studios, 1984.

Parry-Crooke, Charlotte, ed. *Marklin, 1895–1914.* London: Denys Ingram Publishers, 1983.

Pressland, David. *The Art of the Tin Toy.* New York: Crown Publishers, 1976.

Remise, Jac. *L'Argus des Jouets Anciens, 1850–1918.* Balland, 1978.

————, and Fondin, Jean. English text by D. B. Tubbs. *The Golden Age of Toys.* Lausanne: Edita S.A., 1967.

Spong, Neldred and Raymond. *Flywheel Powered Toys.* Antique Toy Collectors of America, 1979.

White, Gwen. *Toys and Dolls, Marks and Labels.* Newton, Mass.: Charles T. Branford Company, 1975.

Whitton, Blair. *American Clockwork Toys, 1862–1900.* Exton, Pa.: Schiffer Publishing, 1981.

Index